WITHDRAWN

Children's Books
OLD AND RARE

WALTER SCHATZKI

Photograph by Fabian Bachrach

CHILDREN'S BOOKS
OLD AND RARE

CATALOGUE NUMBER ONE

Foreword by Leslie Shepard

WALTER SCHATZKI
558 MADISON AVENUE
NEW YORK

Republished by Gale Research Company, Book Tower, Detroit, 1974

Library of Congress Cataloging in Publication Data

Schatzki, Walter, 1899-
    Old and rare children's books.

    Reprint of the 1941 ed. published in New York by the author.
    1. Children's literature--Bibliography--Catalogs. 2. Bibliography--Rare books--Catalogs. I. Title.
Z1037.S33   028.52   73-16044

NEW FOREWORD

The reissue of the present valuable catalogue is a good opportunity to record an appreciation of the compiler, a collector and dealer whose wide knowledge of children's books has been of great assistance to many librarians and private collectors.

WALTER SCHATZKI was born in 1899 near Siegen in southern Westphalia. Throughout his life he has been attracted to both books and music. He became interested in antiquarian books at a very early age. When only eight years old he was staying with his grandparents in a small country town. While playing in their big empty barn he found an old book of fables lying amongst the beams. The book was printed in the eighteenth century and he has never forgotten how it fascinated him at the time. Later, as a high school student, he used to roam around in the local bookshops and help out during the weeks before Christmas. He lived about thirty miles from Cologne. Every month his aunt used to receive a package of books and catalogues from a bookshop and lending library in that city and Schatzki was particularly attracted by the catalogues. They showed a picture of the shop which had six or seven windows. His family had textile interests and even as a child he thought "Why can't we have a bookshop in our town instead of a textile mill?"

His love of music had its beginning at the age of twelve when he heard a concert of the already at that time famous violinist Adolf Busch who also came from Siegen. Schatzki took violin lessons.

When he had finished high school he became an apprentice in a department store, selling fabrics and carpets. This was during the first World War. Before he had finished his apprenticeship, however, he became a soldier. After the war he went to the University of Munich, and then to Frankfurt, where he studied economics for two terms. Like many young men of the time he belonged to the Wandervogel, the youth movement whose members hiked all over Germany, staying at youth hostels, old castles, or in tents, discussing the writings of poets of the German Romantic period like Clemens Brentano and Achim von Arnim, and singing folksongs.

While planning his summer vacation in 1919 he came in contact with a book organization called Wanderbuchhandlung. This organization wanted to bring good books to the people in the countryside who had never seen a bookshop, and they were looking for students to help in this work. This was exactly the job for Schatzki, and so began one of the most romantic episodes of his career.

He became a book pedlar, just like the chapmen of medieval times. He had a pack containing books, and his fiddle. He travelled to towns and villages in the Röhn, a remote central section of Germany, playing the fiddle at country fairs. Crowds would gather round and join in the singing; then Schatzki would bring out his little books for children as well as for grownups, and offer them for sale. When there was no fair he went from house to house on a bicycle. In those days Germany had no rubber for bicycle tires and the wheels had an ingenious arrangement of metal springs instead of tires; of course it was bumpy and made a terrible noise!

At the end of this adventure which lasted for six weeks, Schatzki got a job in the office of the organization for which he had been working, and spent three months learning the whole technical business of the book trade.

Soon afterwards his grandmother died, leaving an inheritance to Schatzki and his brothers. With his share he went to Frankfurt and opened a bookshop of his own in the busiest part of the town center. The shop was named Jugend-Bücher-Stube (Children's Book Store) and specialized in books for children and young people. It was the first bookshop of its kind in Germany. It opened in May 1920 when Schatzki was only twenty years old.

In 1923 he added a rare book department and put his own name over the shop. His first marriage took place soon afterwards. One day, while visiting Munich for a book auction, he browsed around the city and found a large book shop with all kinds of odd things. In one corner was a group of children's books which included the first edition of a German juvenile classic *The Easter Eggs*, a book that was subsequently translated and published many times in nineteenth-century France. This first edition, in original binding, was priced at three marks (75 cents). The thought occured to him that if he could buy important children's books at such prices he had better start collecting them. That was the beginning of his special collections.

One of his early acquisitions was a first edition of the famous *Struwwelpeter* of Heinrich Hoffmann, a book of which only six complete copies are known to have survived. In the twenties and early thirties there were only a few collectors of children's books in Germany, and Schatzki had the field more or less to himself. He was able to assemble a splendid collection. During the depression in the early thirties he was, like many other merchants, in need of funds. It happened that at that time he was asked by a prominent American bookseller to send his collection for an exhibition to New York. Most of the books exhibited had probably never been seen on that side of the ocean, and the collection was eventually bought by the New York Public Library where the Schatzki bookplate on each item is an indication of his good taste and skill in collecting.

A few years afterwards, a book on German children's books was published with many illustrations, most of which came from Schatzki's second collection which he had started after the sale of the first. The author had spent a week with the Schatzki family for his research and, after having finished the book he dedicated it to the memory of Mrs. Schatzki who had died in the meantime.

In the course of the years the Bücherstube (now a shop with seven windows!) had extended its range of interest beyond children's books in the direction of a general bookstore, and had become one of the best known in Germany and, in a way, a cultural center of the city of Frankfurt. However, with the Nazis in power Schatzki was not permitted to continue his work, and he emigrated to the United States in December 1937.

He had to start all over again as a book dealer, but by now his great reputation had preceded him. He was invited to give a lecture to librarians at the New York Public Library where the Schatzki collection of children's books was already highly prized.

He opened a store for old and rare books in New York, where he extended the range of his dealer activities. He became an expert on musical manuscripts and many rare and valuable items passed through his hands. He negotiated the sale of the manuscripts of Beethoven's F Major Quartet (Op. 135) which came from the renowned Hinrichsen collection in Leipzig, the Brahms' First Symphony, and many other key items. Some passed through his hands more than once as collectors changed their collecting interests. His expert judgment was widely sought and he was consulted by leading collectors.

He brought the idea of a collection of children's books to the late Edgar S. Oppenheimer and advised him in his collecting activities. This collection is probably the finest of its kind in private hands, containing about 6500 titles in English (American and British), French, German, Dutch and Italian with almost all the high spots in each language.

In 1943 Schatzki married again; he also became an American citizen. At his present book store on East 57th Street in New York he and Johanna Thomsen, his assistant for many years, are surrounded by charming books, manuscripts, prints, and ephemera relating to a wide field of interest. The store is a treasure-house of the beautiful, unusual, and unique. Today Schatzki is a white-haired distinguished man, an expert to the fingertips, friendly and helpful, and his store one of the most delightful book centers in New York where city redevelopment is unfortunately diminishing so much of the antiquarian book trade.

The present catalogue was first published in 1941, and is now a scarce and little known item in an area of expanding importance to collectors, bibliographers, and librarians. Mr. Frederick G. Ruffner, a Detroit collector who acquired many items from Schatzki, determined to reprint the catalogue. There are still too many gaps in our knowledge of early children's literature and this reprint will be a valuable addition to well-known works like those of Gumuchian, Opie, Muir, and the catalogue of the Osborne Collection.

1973   LESLIE SHEPARD

Children's Books
Old and Rare

CATALOGUE
NUMBER
ONE

WALTER SCHATZKI

558 MADISON AVENUE

NEW YORK

TABLE OF CONTENTS

ABC-BOOKS AND PRIMERS	3
THE ORBIS PICTUS	8
THE BIBLE	11
POETRY—NURSERY RHYMES	13
FAIRY TALES AND FABLES	15
SHAKESPEARE, ROBINSON CRUSOE, GULLIVER, AND DON QUIXOTE	19
THE MORAL TALE	21
THE PICTURE STORY	26
JUVENILE FICTION	30
GAMES AND SPORTS	32
HISTORY AND GEOGRAPHY	34
NATURAL HISTORY	37
PERIODICALS AND ALMANACS	39
MISCELLANEOUS	40
(THE AMERICAN WOODCUT)	41
(FASHIONS AND COSTUMES)	41
BOOKS ABOUT CHILDREN'S BOOKS	41

PLATE I

No. 51. The Juvenile Numerator. 1810

No. 55. Songs for the Nursery. 1822

PLATE II

No. 124. The Butterfly's Ball. 1807
(Original size)

OLD AND RARE
CHILDREN'S BOOKS

OFFERED

FOR SALE

BY

WALTER SCHATZKI

DEALER IN

RARE BOOKS, PRINTS AND AUTOGRAPHS

NEW YORK

558 MADISON AVENUE   PLAZA 5-3016

Prices in this catalogue are net and include carriage. Orders from customers unknown to me should be accompanied by remittance or satisfactory references. All books may be ordered subject to approval and are returnable within eight days.

The Code word for this catalogue is "JUVENILE."

IF YOU ARE NOT INTERESTED IN THE SUBJECT OF THIS CATALOGUE, PLEASE DO NOT THROW IT AWAY BUT PASS IT ON TO ONE OF YOUR FRIENDS.

TO THE
GENTLE READER
AND
PROSPECTIVE BUYER

No. 106

It is with great pleasure that I present to the public my first catalogue of Early Children's Books. When I sold my own collection to the New York Public Library in 1932 (now the "Schatzki Collection of Children's Books"), my interest in this field was quite separate from my activities as a bookseller. However, I continued to devote my attention to this branch of book collecting and, with growing public interest, have made it a special and important part of my work.

In studying the history of the development of children's books it soon becomes evident that they offer as great a variety of types and groups as one would expect to find in books written for adults. In this catalogue I made such a grouping and under each heading I have arranged the items in chronological order. An alphabetical index covering all will be found at the end.

Many libraries, especially in recent years, are giving a large and increasing space to books produced for juveniles; but there is none, so far as I know, that is devoted exclusively to books of this class. Consequently such collections as do exist must necessarily remain fragmentary. Of course, these volumes are usually small and unassuming in appearance and they add little to the development of science and art. But we should remember that also Shakespeare, Rousseau, Goethe, Newton, Washington, and Noah Webster were among those who as children drew their first knowledge of things from them. From these tiny books came to them the first ideas of the beauties of human language and of the facts and poetry they conveyed. As there were no libraries in those days who regarded these books as of sufficient importance to buy them as they came from the press and to put them on their shelves, a great number of them have disappeared. So it has been left to chance to decide which and how many of the little books should last to our time and it was left to the zeal and interest of collectors to save the survivors from destruction and oblivion.

I can imagine a library, devoted solely to this wide field of juvenile literature of all centuries and in all languages. It would probably not duplicate any existing library and would provide an opportunity to study the place and influence that children's books had in their times. They would reflect the minds of the authors who wrote them and the thoughts of the publishers who produced them for the markets; on the one hand the educational ideas that created them and on the other their relative importance to the men who brought them before the world. It is obvious that such a collection would be welcomed today by all who are engaged in the production of books for children—be they writers, illustrators, printers, publishers, or booksellers. And it would not be too much to say, also for those who buy them; for parents, educators, librarians, and even uncles and aunts.

* *

In my descriptions I have abstained from using the term "rare" too frequently. It lies within the nature of a child's book that it will not last long and that it is its fate to be "loved to pieces". Therefore many of the earlier children's books are rare; of a number listed in this catalogue no other copy is known.

The catalogue contains more than forty illustrations. Had it been possible I would have put in many more. These pictures are intended not only to illustrate the books from which they are taken. They are also intended to give a taste or general idea of the abundance and wealth of artistic variety in all the books described in the catalogue.

An asterisk (*) indicates that the illustrations in the book so marked are CONTEMPORARILY colored by hand.

All books are complete and in good condition unless otherwise described. Slight signs of use, light spotting, and inscriptions on fly-leaves have not been specifically mentioned; but any differences from this standard, both better and worse, have been carefully noted. All books may be returned within one week if not satisfactory.

* *

Books about children's books to which has been referred:

DARTON (F. J. H.). Children's Books in England.
GUMUCHIAN ET CIE. Les Livres de l'Enfance.
HALSEY (R. V.). Forgotten Books of the American Nursery.
JAMES (PH.). Children's Books of Yesterday.
ROSENBACH (A. S. W.). Early American Children's Books.
RUEMANN (A.). Alte Deutsche Kinderbücher.
TUER (A. W.). Forgotten Children's Books.
TUER (A. W.). Old-Fashioned Children's Books.

No. 59

ABC-BOOKS AND PRIMERS

1. TABULAE ABCDARIAE PUERILES. Broadside. Small folio. Preserved between boards. (Leipzig, V. Babst, c. 1544). $48.00

Excellently preserved example of an early primer printed on one side of a single sheet. Probably the oldest ABC of its kind and a forerunner of the horn-book. Three alphabets in Latin and Gothic letters, vowels, etc., and the paternoster, are surrounded by a delicately ornamented border. The nature of this border has made it possible to trace the printer of the leaflet. Such single leaves are more exposed to wear and tear than schoolbooks and other juveniles and it is only by happy accident that a few specimens of this primer were found among the files of a record-office in Germany some 15 years ago.— Gumuchian, 1; reproduced in Rümann, Kinderbücher (plate 338).

2. A.B.C. 16pp. Small 8vo. Sewn. Lüneburg, 1701. $18.00

Early German primer. First and last pages printed in black and red. The former shows the ABC in Gothic and Latin letters. On the last page woodcut of a rooster, the symbol of diligence.

[See Illustration on Plate III]

3. A.B.C. 8vo. 16pp. Unopened and uncut. Stargard, bey dem Buchdrucker Hendess (c. 1750). $18.00

Early German primer. Title-page in black and red, as is the last page, which shows a schoolroom with the teacher, sitting at his table, a rod in his hand, surrounded by the children. In the foreground a rooster and two chickens. The rooster was the symbol of diligence.—Gumuchian, 11, with reproduction of the last page.

4. BILDER-A.B.C. mit einigen Lesübungen, Gedenksprüchen und Gebeten für Kinder. 8vo. Marbled boards, red label. Stralsund, 1788. $18.00

Early German primer. The alphabet is illustrated by crude but amusing woodcuts. Each woodcut is accompanied by a moral in verses, e. g.: "Quäle nie ein Thier zum Scherz, denn es fühlt, wie Du, den Schmerz."—One page reproduced in Rümann, Kinderbücher (plate 35).

5. NOUVELLE METHODE D'ENSEIGNER l'A.B.C. et a épeller aux enfans en les amusant par des figures agréables et propres à leur faire des progrès dans la lecture et l'écriture presque sans maitre. 8vo. Original grey wrappers, uncut. Orbe, chez Marianne Mourer, 1791. $26.50

Unusually fine French primer. Engraved vignette title showing a boy and a girl writing at a table. A hand holding a quill is shown underneath. The captions of these two engravings read: "Posture du corps pour écrire" and "Tenue de la plume." There are in addition an engraved frontispiece and 104 engravings on 6 plates.

6. EBERHARD (G. A.). ABC und Lesebuch nach der brauchbarsten und leichtesten Methode modulirt und modernisirt . . . Mit 9 sauber colorirten Kupfern aus der Naturgeschichte. 8vo. Contemporary half calf, gilt fillets and red label on back. Leipzig (c. 1800). $12.00

*With many fine hand-colored engravings on 9 plates illustrating natural history. The alphabet is printed in black and red.

7. CAMPE (J. H.). ABC instructive ou Méthode amusante pour apprendre aux Enfants les Elements de la Langue Françoise. Nouvelle edition considérablement augmentée, avec figures. Small 8vo. Contemporary half calf, gilt fillets on back. La Haye, 1801. $9.50

Rare French primer, the alphabets printed in many different characters. With 6 fine full-page engravings. A certificate with delicate ornamental border, inserted before the half-title, states that this book was awarded to a Dutch boy by his teachers.

8. VOIT (JOH. P.). Schule des Vergnügens für kleine Kinder. 8vo. Contemporary marbled boards (somewhat chipped). Nürnberg, 1803. $28.00

*Abundantly illustrated book which combines a primer and a reader. The alphabet is accompanied by 25 large hand-colored engravings; the second part is adorned with 50 hand-colored engravings on 7 plates.—Rümann, Kinderbücher, 348.

[See Illustration on Plate XII]

9. (SPLITTEGARD, CARL FR.). Neues Bilder ABC oder deutsches Lesebuch für die Jugend mit fünf und zwanzig Kupfern. Neue verbesserte Auflage. 8vo. Marbled wrappers, uncut. Vienna and Prag, 1807. $12.00

Engraved title-page with charming engraving of a family scene in a garden and 24 engravings on 12 plates, illustrating the alphabet. Recently colored by hand.

10. ALPHABET RÉCRÉATIF orné de 26 Gravures. 12mo. Contemporary colored wrappers. Paris, 1810. $7.50

French primer with charming vignette on the engraved title-page and 24 engravings of animals (on 6 plates) accompanying the alphabet. A portrait of a child whose life is described at the end is not present.

11. KIMBER AND CONRAD'S ABC BOOK, with Pictures for Children. 16mo. Original wrappers. Philadelphia (c. 1810).

With 41 quaint woodcuts.—Rosenbach, 420. $9.00

12. THE NEW-ENGLAND PRIMER, improved. For the more easy attaining the true Reading of English. To which is added the Assembly of Divines' Catechism. 16mo. Original wrappers (show signs of use). Hartford, Hudson and Goodwin, 1812. $15.00

With woodcuts. Heartman, 250, lists only one copy at Bates College.

13. THE NEW-ENGLAND PRIMER; or, an easy and pleasant Guide to the Art of Reading. Adorned with Cuts. To which is added the Catechism. 16mo. Marbled paper wrappers. Walpole, N. H., I. Thomas and Co., 1814. $12.00

With frontispiece and woodcuts in the text. The title is particularly well printed within a decorative border. Heartman, 270. Rosenbach, 502.

14. SELBIGER (FRIEDR.). Neues ABC, Lese- und Unterhaltungsbuch zur Entwicklung der Seelenkräfte der Jugend beiderlei Geschlechts. Mit 9 ausgemalten Kupfern von Meno Haas. Small 8vo. Original pictorial boards. Berlin, 1818. $15.00

*The 9 full-page plates are of a fine quality and elaborately colored by hand. The very well preserved binding is an excellent example of a publisher's binding of the early romantic period.

15. REINHARDT (J. G.). Nieuw en volkomen A.B.C. Spel- en Talkundig Leesboek voor Kinderen; naar het Hoogduitsch. Met Platen. Derde Druk. Small 8vo. Original printed green wrappers. Zalt-Boemel, 1818. $9.50

*Dutch primer with 24 hand-colored engravings on 6 plates, depicting all kinds of trades and professions, e. g.: a physician, a sculptor, a tailor, a butcher, etc., etc.

16. A.B.C. Small 8vo. Original boards covered with ornamental end-papers. Waldenburg (c. 1820). $8.00

*German primer. With 46 amusing hand-colored woodcut illustrations.

17. ABÉCÉDAIRE et Choix de Lecture pour l'Enfance, avec figures.—Französiches ABC-und Lesebüchlein für Kinder, mit Kupfern. 12mo. Original boards. Pirna (c. 1820). $6.00

*German-French primer with 17 fine hand-colored engravings on 5 plates, showing animals and country scenes.

5

18. THE HISTORY OF AN APPLE PIE. Written by Z. 8vo. Original printed wrappers with woodcut. London, Harris and Son, 1823. $16.50

*In alphabetical order. With hand-colored vignette on title and 13 hand-colored half-page woodcuts. "C cried for it, J jumped over it, M mourned for it, Y yawned for it," etc.—Similar to Gumuchian I bis.

19. A WAS AN APPLE. 16mo. Stitched. New York, Mahlon Day (c. 1830). $4.50

A.B.C. with 25 fine woodcuts. Device on title:
>"O, what a pretty little book!
>So full of pictures, too;
>I should like through it to look;
>I'll buy it—wouldn't you?"

20. THE COMIC ALPHABET. 8vo. 13 leaves printed on one side only, loose in pictorial polychrome wrappers. London, J. Graham (c. 1830). $18.00

Amusing pictorial ABC engraved throughout in aquatint manner. The artist has signed each engraving "R. E. Sly."

[SEE ILLUSTRATION ON PLATE V]

21. SCHOPPE (AMALIE). Kleines Schatzkästlein. Das liebste Lesebuch fleissiger und artiger Kinder. . . . Small 8vo. Original printed boards. Leipzig (c. 1830). $10.00

*With 9 charming hand-colored engravings on 5 plates, showing in alphabetical order 24 tradesmen, soldiers, etc., in their attractive costumes.

22. VATERLANDSCH A.B. BOEK, of Trekken en Markwaardigheden uit de Vaderlandsche Geschiedenis . . . Met 24 Prent-Afbeeldingen. 12mo. Original pictorial boards. Haarlem, 1833. $7.50

*Charming Dutch ABC book with 24 hand-colored engravings on 12 plates, illustrating outstanding events in the history of the Netherlands.

23. GUTMANN (JOHANNES). Leseconfect oder muntere Erzählungen zu Nutz' und Lehr' der lieben Kinderwelt. Mit 24 fein illuminierten Abbildungen. 8vo. Original boards. Nürnberg (c. 1835). $25.00

*Pictorial ABC book, the 24 delightfully hand-colored illustrations for the alphabet printed on 8 plates.

24. CHILD'S ILLUMINATED ALPHABET. 12mo. Folding sheet of 48 inches length, printed pink boards. Springfield, P. D. Reed and Co. (c. 1845). $8.50

*Pictorial ABC printed in blue and colored by hand.

PLATE III

No. 45. Bilderbibel. (C. 1750)

No. 2. A.B.C. 1701

PLATE IV

No. 77. Cruikshank. The Fairy Library

25. **ALPHABET CARICATURE, DIABOLIQUE ET GROTESQUE.** Small 8vo. Folding sheet of 54 inches length, in original hand-colored pictorial boards. Paris (c. 1850). $18.00

*Contains 3 excellently drawn lithographed alphabets colored by hand and I in silhouette. The 110 amusing little pictures display, among others: an artist, an angler, a dentist (parrot and crocodile), acrobats, an orator, drunkards, a tennis-playing hoopoe, etc.

[See Illustration on Plate V]

26. **BLOEMEN EN BLADEN.** Letterkransje voor Lieve Kinderen. Met platen. Small 8vo. Original red cloth, front cover gilt. Groningen (c. 1850). $12.00

*Delightful Dutch ABC book. One letter to a page, each illustrated by three hand-colored subjects. Except for the title and the introductory poem of two pages, the book is engraved throughout. In mint condition.

27. **EMY.** Alphabet illustré de seize dessins. Oblong small 8vo. Original pictorial polychrome boards. Paris (c. 1855). $9.50

*With 29 fine hand-colored lithographs on 16 plates.

27a. **THE ILLUSTRATED ABC,** with Original Engravings. 8vo. Sewn. Troy, Merriam, Moore and Co., 1856. $6.00

*With 7 hand-colored woodcuts.

28. **MONROE'S PRIMARY READING CHARTS.** First Steps in Reading. Elephant folio (30 by 25 inches). 14 leaves kept together at the top edges by a wooden ledge. Philadelphia, Cowperswait and Co., 1877. $35.00

With pictorial title, 23 large woodcuts and one page displaying a color-scale. These mammoth ABC charts were used in the classroom. "Hints for the teacher" are printed on the lower margin of each page. Difficult to find in good condition.

29. **GREENAWAY (KATE).** An Apple Pie. Engraved and printed by Edmund Evans. Original bluish-green pictorial cloth. London (1886). $12.50

This ABC of the Apple Pie ranks high among Kate Greenaway's works. First edition in the first binding.

30. **GREENAWAY (KATE).** Alphabet. 32mo. Original pictorial boards. London and New York (c. 1890). $1.50

Charming little alphabet printed in colors from woodblocks engraved by Edmund Evans. Each page carries one capital letter with a little girl or boy playing around it. In mint condition.

THE ORBIS PICTUS

The publication of "Orbis Sensualism Pictus" by J. A. Comenius (Nürnberg, 1657) marks the beginning of juvenile literature in its own right. Except for ABCs and Catechisms no book especially written for children had ever been published before. The title of the first English edition (1659) reads: "Visible World; or, a picture and nomenclature of all the chief things that are in the world . . . a work newly written by the author in Latin . . . and translated into English . . . for the Use of young Latin-Scholars". The book, profusely illustrated with instructive woodcuts, is a sort of encyclopaedia for juvenile readers which combines the teaching of Latin with the conveyance of the knowledge of almost everything in the world. The "Orbis Pictus" set a pattern for hundreds of books published during the following centuries and in many cases the very title was retained.

31. LA PORTE DES LANGUES. Introduction nouvelle a la Francoise et a la Flamande.—Nieuwe Inleydinge tot de Franse, en Duytse Tale. . . . Small 8vo. Contemporary full calf. Amsterdam, 1686.
$24.00

Early French-Dutch juvenile of the Orbis Pictus type. The publisher refers in his introduction to Comenius. Engraved frontispiece and over 200 engravings on 35 plates. One leaf with two plates missing. Any Orbis Pictus in any language before 1700 is of the utmost rarity.

[SEE ILLUSTRATION ON PLATE IX]

32. NEUER ORBIS PICTUS für Kinder in fünf Sprachen. Ersteszwölftes Heft. 4to. Contemporary half calf (back label partly missing). Leipzig (1788).
$28.00

Copiously illustrated juvenile encyclopaedia in five languages. The 576 engravings on 48 plates convey a good idea of utensils and other articles of daily use during the second half of the eighteenth century, e. g.: hourglass, candlestick, woman's hat, cradle, saw, sun-dial, spectacles, balloon, sewing-frame, etc., etc.

33. NEUE BILDER GALERIE für junge Söhne und Töchter zur angenehmen und nützlichen Selbstbeschäftigung aus dem Reiche der Natur, Kunst, Sitten und des gemeinen Lebens. . . . 14. vols. 8vo. Contemporary mottled calf, red leather labels, gilt backs. Berlin, 1794-1806.
$55.00

*Copious juvenile encyclopaedia with 14 hand-colored vignettes on the engraved title-pages and c. 2000 hand-colored engravings on 277 plates.

34. **LEDERER (JOH. GEORG).** Der kleine Lateiner oder gemeinnützige Kenntnisse aus der Natur und Kunst in der Gestalt eines neuen lateinischen Lesebuchs für Kinder . . . Vierte verbesserte Auflage. Small 8vo. Marbled boards. Nürnberg, 1802. $18.00

*An engraved pictorial title, preceding the printed title, reads: "Die Gemalte Welt oder der gemeinnützige Lateiner." "Gemalte Welt" is the German translation for "Orbis pictus" and the publisher tells us in the preface that Comenius' famous book was his pattern. The Latin text of each of the 76 articles is followed by a Latin-German vocabulary. Among the 47 hand-colored plates there are the printer's shop, the bookbinder, the papermaker, a kitchen, musical instruments, optical instruments, etc., etc. The illustrations are still those of the first edition, published about 1750, and therefore of considerable historical interest. The book is in fair condition, two pages show repairs with loss of a few words. Very rare. The engraved title is reproduced in Rümann, Kinderbücher (plate 219).

No. 35

35. **BERTIN (T. P.).** Le Passe-Temps de l'Enfance, ou le premier Livre élémentaire; Recueil encyclopédique, instructif et amusant, mis à la portée du premier et du second âge. . . . Traduction de l'Anglais. 4 vols. bound in 2. 12mo. Contemporary red half morocco, gilt back. Paris, 1810. $35.00

Very interesting juvenile encyclopaedia with 96 full-page engravings. They include: tools, dishes, costumes, animals, birds, flowers, nursery scenes, games, trades, etc., etc. This book is an adaption in dialogue after a translation of "Löhr. Erste Lehren und Bilder," published in Leipzig in 1805. The editor obviously was not unaware of this fact for he writes in the preface that he believes the original to be English, but he adds this footnote: "Fût il allemand, il n'en devrait pas moin prévenier en sa faveur, car l'Allemagne a fourni depuis quelque temps des ouvrages d'éducation très-recherchés; il suffit de citer ceux de Campe." Apparently, in spite of the war between France and England at that time, it was more fashionable to publish translations from the English than from the German. The binder has used the title-page of Part II for the second volume and omitted those of the two last parts.

[SEE ILLUSTRATION ON PAGE 9]

36. SEIDEL (H.). Neuer Orbis Pictus in sechs Sprachen, oder unterhaltendes und belehrendes Bilderbuch für Kinder von jedem Alter. Fünfte verb. Auflage. Oblong 12mo. Contemporary marbled boards. Nürnberg, 1810. $12.50

*With 40 hand-colored plates depicting 172 varied objects, such as flowers, animals, ships, buildings, tools, furniture, etc.

37. FUNKE (C. PHIL.). Familien-Bilder-Buch zur angenehmen und lehrreichen Unterhaltung der Jugend. Zweite verbesserte Auflage. 8vo. Boards with cloth back, two pictorial sheets (c. 1850) with hand-colored engravings pasted on both covers. Nürnberg, 1812. $15.00

*This book is a sort of family encyclopaedia of the best orbis pictus type. The 155 hand-colored engravings (on 32 plates) are partly identical with those of No. 36 of this catalogue.

38. EENIGE VOORSTELLINGEN van Natur-en Kunstvoorwerpen ... Met Platen. 2 vols. Oblong small 8vo. Original printed boards. Amsterdam (c. 1820). $9.50

*Dutch juvenile of the Orbis Pictus type with about 100 hand-colored engravings on 19 plates, which are copies of the illustrations of No. 36 of this catalogue. The pictures are described in four languages. In mint condition.

39. LEERZAM TIJDVERDRIJF voor de Jeugd ... Met tien gekleurde plaatjes. Square 12mo. Original printed yellow boards. Leyden, 1821. $13.50

*Instructive juvenile with 38 pleasant hand-colored engravings on 10 plates. Many trades, occupations and objects are represented, among them: The making of a sail, demonstrating the whole process from the harvesting of the Flax through spinning and dyeing to the sewing of the cloth. (6 plates). Another plate shows a ship-yard and still another one depicts the **appearance of a** comet and a sun and moon eclipse. In mint condition.

40. MEYNIER (JOH. HEINR.). Neuer Orbis Pictus in deutscher und französischer Sprache ... Dritte verbesserte Auflage. 8vo. Contemporary marbled boards. Nürnberg, 1822. $10.00

*The 10 plates of this volume depict on 60 hand-colored engravings 207 different objects, to be found at home, in the city, in the village, and in the wide world. The pictures give a good idea of the tools, furniture, dresses, etc., of the times 120 years back.

PLATE V

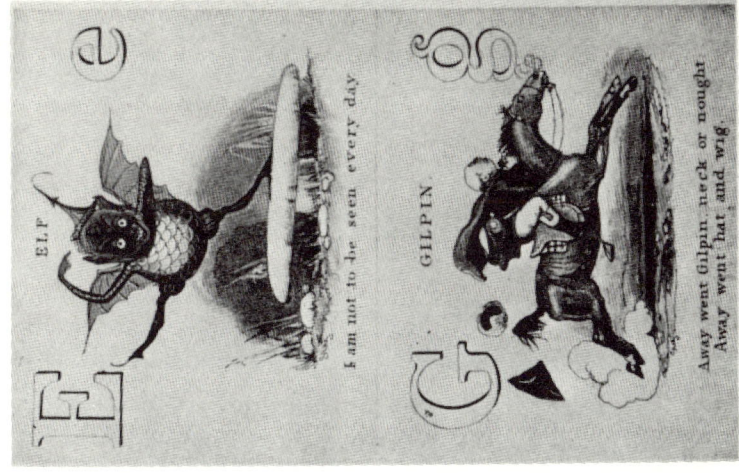

No. 20. The Comic Alphabet. (C. 1830)

No. 25. Alphabet Caricature. (C. 1850)

PLATE VI

No. 139

No. 49

40a. FLETCHER (W.). The Picturesque Primer; or, Useful Matter Made Pleasing Pastime for Leisure Hours. Small 8vo. Contemporary half roan. London (1828). $20.00

*With 120 delicate wood-engravings on 18 plates, elaborately colored by hand. The different pictures on each plate are partitioned by garlands of various flowers.—Gumuchian, 126.

[See Illustration on Plate XIII]

41. GAILER (J. E.). Neuer Orbis Pictus für die Jugend, oder Schauplatz der Natur, der Kunst und des Menschenlebens in 316 lithographierten Abbildungen mit genauer Erklärung in deutscher, lateinischer und französischer Sprache nach der früheren Auflage des Comenius bearbeitet und dem jetzigen Zeitbedürfnisse gemäss eingerichtet. Small 4to. Old half calf. Stuttgart, 1832. $20.00

FIRST EDITION of the best German 19th Century Orbis Pictus in German, Latin and French. The skillfully drawn lithographs, 316 on 158 plates, represent everything that can be expected in a juvenile manual of this type. Two full-page illustrations show two boys with their teacher.—Rümann, Kinderbücher, 120.

[See Illustration on Page 12]

42. NEUE SYSTEMATISCHE BILDERSCHULE für das Jugendalter. Der Bilderschule zweiter Teil, eingeleitet von Friedrich Güll. . . . Mit 18 colorierten Bildertafeln in Tondruck. Folio. Original printed boards. Nürnberg (c. 1838). $12.00

*With decorative hand-colored title and 156 brilliantly hand-colored lithographs on 18 plates They include: trades, costumes, ships, animals, country scenes, elemental catastrophies, etc.

43. MARTIN (WILLIAM). The Parlour Book; or, Familiar Conversations on Science and the Arts. Small square 8vo. Original pictorial cloth. London (c. 1845). $12.00

*With 16 hand-colored full-page lithographs displaying: filling of a balloon, a ship-yard, launching of a ship, a diving bell, etc. The pictures are surrounded by instructive designs of technical details. The text is written in the form of conversations in the Peter Parley style.—Gumuchian, 3986. James, Children's Books of Yesterday, p. 92.

THE BIBLE

44. KERN UND AUSZUG DES BUCHES JESUS SIRACH, . . . Der Jugend zur Lust und Erweckung, mit schönen, die Hauptwörter ausdrückenden Bildern gezieret. Small 8vo. Boards, red label. Nürnberg, 1734. $15.00

With 28 engraved full-page plates, containing verses of the bible which are adorned with delicate pictures substituting many words within the text. One page reproduced in Rümann, Kinderbücher (plate 199).

45. CURIEUSE BILDER-BIBEL oder die vornehmsten Sprüche der heiligen Schrift in Figuren vorgestellt wodurch dieselben der zarten Jugend aud eine angenehme u. ergötzende Art bekanna gemacht werden können. Small 8vo. Marbled boards. Nürnberg (c. 1750). $15.00

*Early hieroglyphical Bible. Engraved title and frontispiece and hundreds of handcolored woodcuts throughout the text. Some pages repaired with loss of a few letters. One page reproduced in Rümann, Kinderbücher (plate 39).

[SEE ILLUSTRATION ON PLATE III]

46. A CURIOUS HIEROGLYPHICK BIBLE; or, Select Passages in the Old and New Testaments, represented with emblematical Figures, for the Amusement of Youth . . . 12mo. Original pictorial boards, backstrip reinforced. London, 1796. $12.00

With hundreds of woodcuts which have been attributed to Bewick. This is the 13th edition. Gumuchian lists the tenth edition of 1791.

47. KLEINE BILDER-BIBEL FUER KINDER.—Petite Bible en estampes à l'usage de la jeunesse. 8vo. Blue boards. Vienna (c. 1820). $7.50

*With eight handcolored plates depicting 48 scenes from the Bible.

48. BIJBELSCH PRENTGESCHENK VOOR KINDEREN. Met 94 fraaije Houtgravuren. 12mo. Original printed boards. Amsterdam, 1844. $6.00

*With 94 handcolored full-page woodcuts.

No. 41

POETRY—NURSERY RHYMES

49. A COLLECTION OF PRETTY POEMS for the Amusement of Children Six Foot High. Interspersed with a Series of Letters from Cousin Sam to Cousin Sue, on the Subjects of Criticism, Poetry, and Politics. With Notes Variorum. Calculated with a Design to do good. ... 16mo. Original flowered Dutch paper boards (chipped and rubbed, rebacked). In half morocco slip-case. London, Printed for the Booksellers of Europe, Asia, Africa and America; and sold at the Bible and Sun in St. Paul's Church-yard (J. Newbery), 1757.
$75.00

This little book, adorned with 9 amusing full page engravings (possibly by Francis Hayman), is, as the title indicates, not a book for children. But it was published by Newbery in the same style, the same size, and the same binding as his juvenile books. The title is inspired by Thomas Tagg's "Collection of Pretty Poems for the Amusement of Children Three Foot High". Besides some anonymous poems the book contains poems by Gray, Swift, Tagg, a.o.
The long satirical foot-notes which form an essential part of the little work give some reason to conjecture that *Oliver Goldsmith* has something to do with its writing. In connection with this the following quotation from the introduction of "Goody Two-Shoes" may be of some importance: "Do you intend this for Children, Mr. Newberry? Why, do you suppose this is written by Mr. Newberry, Sir? This may come from another Hand. This is not the Book mentioned in the Title but the Introduction to that Book, and it is intended, Sir, not for those Sort of Children, but for Children of six Foot high, of which, as my friend justly observed, there are many Millions in the Kingdom". Moreover, "an author who wrote for children six foot high" is mentioned in an essay "Thoughts upon Trade" published in 1760 in Nr. 19 of "The Public Ledger".
Charles Welsh never saw a copy of this FIRST EDITION. He lists the Bodleian copy of 1770 and cites a 1758 edition mentioned in a Newbery catalogue without having seen a copy. Gumuchian 2771 is dated 1779.

[SEE ILLUSTRATION ON PLATE VI]

50. WATTS (I.). Divine Songs, attempted in easy language, for the use of children. ... Adorned with thirty-seven elegant cuts ... 12mo. Flowered Dutch paper boards. London, G. Gower (c. 1790).
$16.50

The 37 woodcuts are of a fine quality in the best Newbery tradition. Gumuchian lists a similar edition (5789 bis). See Darton, Children's Books, pages 106-12.

51. THE JUVENILE NUMERATOR. Square 12mo. Original blue wrappers. In half morocco slip-case. London, Stevens and Co., July 1st, 1810.
$48.00

*Engraved throughout and brightly colored by hand. Frontispiece, pictorial title and 10 delightful full-page pictures illustrating the Nursery Rhyme "One two, buckle my shoe—Three four, open the door—etc.". Unrecorded early, if not first, printing of these famous verses well-known to every child. The text differs in some places from other printings. "Eleven twelf," for instance, rhymes in the collection of the Everyman's Library on "dig and delve" while it reads here " a cat on the shelf". In mint condition.

[SEE ILLUSTRATION ON PLATE I]

52. FOOD FOR THE MIND; or, A New Riddle Book: Compiled for the Use of the great and the little good Boys and Girls in the United States of America. By Jack the Giant Killer, Esq. ... 12mo.

Original printed blue wrappers with three woodcuts (rebacked and wrappers soiled). Albany, H. C. Southwick, 1813. $9.50

Amusing riddle book with 60 rather crude but impressive woodcuts. Rosenbach lists no American edition of this famous juvenile that was first published by Newbery of London about 1760 and reprinted many times through the 18th and 19th century in England and America. The book shows signs of frequent use and the proud little owner of 125 years ago whose name was Henry Yates has inscribed it three times on the fly-leaves: "Steal not this book for fear of shame, for fear you will see the owner's name".

53. OLD GRAND-PAPA, and other Poems, for the Amusement of Children. By a young Lady. Embellished with good Engravings. 8vo. Original wrappers. Philadelphia, B. Warner, 1817. $18.00

With 22 large size woodcuts of a very fine quality probably by A. Anderson. A poem on the four quarters of the worlds ends:

> In Africa are tawny Moors,
> In Europe we have fops and boors,
> In Asia once liv'd Prester John,
> America had Washington.

[See Illustration on Plate XIV]

54. ALPHEN (H. VAN). Kleine Gedichten vor Kinderen. 12mo. Contemporary half red morocco, gilt fillets and black label. Utrecht, 1821. $15.00

With portrait of the author, engraved title and 66 full-page engravings depicting scenes of children at home, on the street, and in the garden. The illustrations convey a good idea of Dutch family life of that time. With the autograph signature of the publisher J. G. Van Terveen.

55. SONGS FOR THE NURSERY, collected from the works of the most renowned poets, and adapted to favorite national melodies. Square 12mo. Full calf. London, Darton, 1822. $20.00

With 24 charming full-page engravings. The first edition was published in 1818. James, Children's books of yesterday p. 68. Gumuchian 5406 lists an edition of 1825.

[See Illustration on Plate I]

57. MAHLON DAY. Twenty-three juvenile booklets published by Mahlon Day of New York in 1829. 16mo. Bound together in one volume. Contemporary half roan, gilt back (binding loose). $48.00

Interesting collection of toy-books printed by the noted publisher of juveniles, either bound up by a private buyer or distributed by the publisher himself in this form as a sort of "Omnibus-Book". Included among the titles in the volume are: "The Rhyming Alphabet. Tales for Thomas. New Riddle Book. The Babes in the Wood. The New-York Cries in Rhyme. Little Susan and her Lamb". With hundreds of woodcuts. Some of the titles are listed in Rosenbach under different dates. The famous New-York Cries have recently been reprinted by Grosset and Dunlap.

[See Illustration on Plate VIII]

58. THE HOUSE THAT JACK BUILT. (The entertaining story of). Small 8vo. Loose in pink paper wrappers. New York, George Burgess (c. 1830). $15.00

*Pictorial title and 10 full-page illustrations with text, engraved throughout and printed on one side only. Delightfully colored by hand. Rosenbach lists and reproduces a similar book by the same publisher (758).

PLATE VII

No. 149. Guths Muths.
Gymnastics. 1800

No. 99. Salzmann.
Elements of Morality. 1791

PLATE VIII

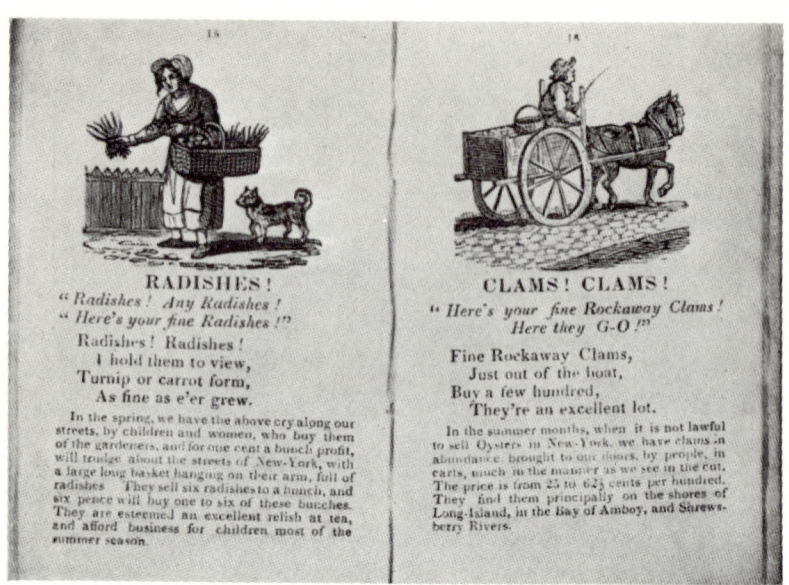

No. 57. The New York Cries. 1829

No. 97. A Pretty New Year's Gift. 1786

58a. THE PROGRESS OF INDUSTRY. Small 8vo. Original pictorial wrappers. (London, c. 1830). $4.50

*With 8 fine hand-colored woodcuts.

59. FEST-KALENDER von Fr. G. Pocci, G. Görres und ihren Freunden. 15 Hefte. 4to. Bound in one volume, original pictorial boards. München und Wien (1835-37). $48.00

Contains religious and regular poems, many accompanied by music. Lithographed throughout and copiously illustrated by Pocci of the most gifted and prolific illustrators of the German Romantic period), Kaulbach, Steinle, Grimm, a.o. 120 leaves, almost all of which are printed on one side only. The two first parts in second edition. Some of the original wrappers bound in. Rümann, Kinderbücher 268.

[SEE ILLUSTRATIONS ON PAGE 3 AND ON FRONT COVER OT THIS CATALOGUE]

60. MOTHER GOOSE'S MELODIES. The only Pure Edition. Containing all that have come to light of her memorable writings, together with those which have been discovered among the Mss. of Herculaneum. . . . The whole compared, revised, and sanctioned, by one of the annotators of the Goose Family. (Copyright 1833). Square small 12mo. Original purple cloth, yellow printed label on front cover. Boston, Munroe and Francis (c. 1838). $25.00

*The different editions of this famous American book of nursery rhymes are very elusive. All editions published after 1833 have the copyright notice of that year. The first edition was published in 1824 but all editions before 1840 are difficult to find in good condition. The numerous woodcuts are carefully colored by hand. See Rosenbach 784 and 801 and the erratum notice on page 355.

FAIRY TALES AND FABLES

61. LES FABLES ET LA VIE D'ESOPE, en François et Allemand, pour l'utilité et recreation de ceux qui se plaisent esdites deux langues, ou qui les veulent apprendre. 12mo. Boards. (Lyon), Jean de Tournes, 1606. $15.00

Curious edition in two languages, French and German, printed in two columns. One part of the introduction (printed in civilité letters) reads: "... maie aussi enrichie par la version Allemande, que nous mise á costé de la Françoise, á l'aide d'un docte jeune homme, natif d'Eidelberg, qui m'a faict ce plaisir de traduire ces fables . . .". With many woodcuts by Bernard Salomon, called "Le petit Bernard", which were first used in a French edition of Esope in 1547. Title page a little frayed.

62. MOTHER BUNCH'S FAIRY TALES. Published for the Amusement of all Little Masters and Misses . . . — Christmas Tales. For the Instruction of Good Boys and Girls, by Mr. Solomon Sobersides. — A Selection of Stories; containing the History of the two Sisters, the Fisherman . . . 12mo. Old half calf, gilt back. Glasgow, Lumsden (c. 1805). $12.00

Three separate publications bound together. With 21 full-page engravings, printed in green and brown. The first booklet is listed by Gumuchian (No. 4205).

63. KLEINE FABELWELT für kleine Leute oder Sammlung der schönsten und lehrreichsten Fabeln für die Jugend. Mit vielen Kupfern. Small square 8vo. Original printed wrappers (binding a little loose and the covers rubbed). Nürnberg u. Leipzig bei Friedrich Campe, 1806. $24.00

*With engraved pictorial title and 19 full-page handcolored engravings of unusual charm. Rümann, Kinderbücher 107.

64. GRIMM (ALBERT LUDWIG). Mährchen-Bibliothek für Kinder. Aus den Mährchen alter Zeiten und Völker ausgewählt und erzählt. 7 vols. 12mo. Contemporary half calf, gilt and tooled back. Frankfurt a.M., 1820-26. $35.00

Vols. 1-5: Mährchen der Tausend und eine Nacht (Arabian Nights); vols. 6-7: Märchen der alten Griechen und Romer. This set represents one of the earliest adaptions of the Arabian Nights for children. A complete set is extremely rare, especially in the fine condition of the present set. Each volume has a delightful engraving by Ramberg. One illustration is reproduced in Rümann, Kinderbücher (plate 142).

65. THE COURT OF OBERON; or, Temple of the Fairies: A Collection of Tales of Past Times. Originally related by Mother Goose, Mother Bunch, and Others, adapted to the language and manners of the present period. 8vo. Full calf, gilt. London, Harris, 1823. $30.00

*Collection of 28 of the most famous fairy-tales as: Little Riding-hood; Blue-Beard; Cinderella; The Story of Fortunio; Beauty and the Beast; Alladin and the Wonderlamp; etc. Adorned with 24 full-page engravings delightfully colored by hand.

GERMAN

POPULAR STORIES,

TRANSLATED FROM THE

RINDER UND HANS MÄRCHEN,

COLLECTED

By M. M. GRIMM,
From Oral tradition.

BOSTON:
CUMMINGS, HILLIARD, AND COMPANY
1826.

No. 66

66. GRIMM (WILHELM AND JACOB). German Popular Stories, translated from the Rinder und Hans Märchen (sic), collected by M. M. Grimm. From Oral tradition. 12mo. Contemporary marbled boards, red leather back and corners, gilt fillets on back (somewhat chipped and rubbed). Boston, Cummings, Hilliard and Company, 1826. $75.00

FIRST AMERICAN EDITION of these famous fairy tales. Evidently a reprint of vol. I of the first English edition illustrated by Cruikshank, (2 vols., London, 1823-26).

The pagination goes from 4 to 13, omitting 5 to 12; but these pages were almost certainly never printed. In the London edition the pages contain the preface which the American editor, perhaps in a last-minute decision, has omitted entirely. The omission among the "Notes" at the end of the volume of a note

referring to the preface seems to prove that the omission of the preface was intentional. A further confirmation of this is the physical condition of the book.
Tear in title-page repaired. Upper fifth of half-title cut off without affecitng the text. Front fly-leaf missing. Inscriptions to and by C. P. A. Burnett with his book-plate on inner side of front cover.
NOT RECORDED BY ANY BIOGRAPHER. NO OTHER COPY HAS BEEN LOCATED.

[SEE REPRODUCTION OF TITLE PAGE]

67. HAZEU (J.). Fabelen uit het Dierenrijk, in Dichtmaat. Voor onderzoekende Kinderen. Small 8vo. Original printed boards. Amsterdam, 1830. $12.00

*With hand-colored pictorial title and 24 delightful hand-colored woodcut-vignettes. In mint condition.

68. SAMMLUNG VON FABELN und Erzählungen aus vaterländischen Dichtern. Ein Geschenk für die Jugend. Mit 16 illuminierten Bildern. Small 8vo. Original printed boards. Berlin (c. 1835). $8.50

Charming book of fables with 16 elaborately hand-colored full-page lithographs. One picture reproduced in Rümann, Kinderbücher (plate 297).

69. LE LIVRE DES ENFANTS. Contes des Fées. 2 vols. Small 8vo. Contemporary half calf, gilt back. Stuttgart, 1839. $12.00

Collection of the most famous fairy tales. With 40 lithographed full-page illustrations.

70. AESOP'S FABLES, with upwards of One Hundred and Fifty Emblematical Devices. 12mo. Original gilt red morocco. Philadelphia, Thomas, Cowperthwait and Co., 1839. $6.00

With 150 fine wood-engravings heading the fables.

71. SNEEWITTCHEN. Ein Kindermärchen. Mit 17 Bildern. Small 8vo. Original wrappers with pictorial hand-colored front cover. Berlin (c. 1845). $7.50

*The 17 hand-colored lithographs of half-page size are by Theodor Hosemann and are considered among his finest. This artist illustrated more than 200 children's books. Title-page reproduced in Rümann, Kinderbücher (plate 325).

72. LES MILLE ET UNE NUITS. Contes chosis. Alladin, Ali Baba, Ali Cogia. Revus pour les enfants. 8vo. Original polychrome boards (little worn and binding loose). Paris (c. 1845).
$6.00

*French translation of "Arabian Nights," with 12 fine hand-colored full-page engravings.

73. MUSAEUS (J. K. A.). Volksmährchen der Deutschen. Prachtausgabe in einem Bande. . . . . Mit Holzschnitten nach Originalzeichnungen von L. Richter, G. Osterwald u. a. und 12 grösseren Titelblättern von L. Richter. 4to. Three-quarter morocco. Leipzig, 1845. $22.50

The first edition of 1842 with a new title-page. Apparently the first edition did not sell very well; therefore the publisher added in this edition 12 fullpage lithographs after drawings by Ludwig Richter. This book, adorned with over 250 delightful woodcuts, 151 of which are by Richter, is one of the most beautifully illustrated works of the romantic period in Germany.

[SEE ILLUSTRATION ON PAGE 22]

74. ANDERSON (HANS CHR.). Story Book: with A Memoir by Mary Howitt, and Illustrations. Small 8vo. Original pictorial gilt green cloth. New York, Francis and Co., 1849. $7.50

Early American edition. Three parts, with separate pagination, bound in one volume of over 500 pages. With the author's portrait, 3 full-page woodcut illustrations and some smaller woodcut vignettes.

75. PERRAULT (CHARLES). Les Contes des Fées. Précédés d'une notice sur l'auteur par Elisabeth Müller. 8vo. Pictorial chromo lithographic boards (a little worn). Paris (c. 1850). $8.00

*With 10 hand-colored full-page engravings and many woodcut vignettes.

76. PERRAULT (CHARLES). Contes des Fées. 12mo. Pictorial hand-colored boards. Paris (c. 1850). $5.00

*With woodcut vignettes and four hand-colored lithographed plates.

77. CRUIKSHANK (GEORGE). Fairy Library. Genuine proofs of the plates on India Paper. (1) Hop-o'-my-Thumb and the Seven League Boots; (2) Jack and the Beanstalk; (3) Cinderella; and (4) Puss in Boots. In all, 39 subjects on 24 plates. Small 4to. Full dark green morocco, gilt inside border, title on front cover and back, by Zaehnsdorf with his special mark. (London, 1853-64). $580.00

First issue of these charming plates of great interest and rarity. They are from George Cruikshank's own collection. Exceptionally brilliant impressions. The first three titles, written in ink, are in Cruikshank's own hand and bear his bold signature. The six plates of the fourth volume are each signed separately in pencil: "First Proof. George Cruikshank."

[SEE ILLUSTRATION ON PLATE IV]

77a. THE FABLES OF AESOP AND OTHERS. Translated into Human Nature. Designed and Drawn on the Wood by Charles H. Bennett. Engraved by Swain. 4to. Original pictorial boards. London, 1857). $10.00

*The 22 full-page woodcuts are carefully colored by hand. One plate reproduced in James, Children's Books of Yesterday (p. 109).

78. MAERCHEN UND SAGEN für Jung und Alt. ... Mit 24 Illustrationen. 4to. Original cloth. Düsseldorf (c. 1857). $13.50

The 24 full-page two-tone lithographs are by the best artists of the Düsseldorf-school as: Sonderland. Schrödter, Scheuren, Oppenheim, a.o.

79. ANDERSEN (HANS CHR.). Wonderful Tales from Denmark. A new translation with illustrations. 8vo. Original pictorial cloth. New York, James Miller, 1864. $6.50

With 6 full-page woodcuts and many woodcut vignettes. At the end 8 pages of advertisements.

80. BLUE-BEARD. Pantomime Toy Book. 4to. Original pictorial polychrome boards. New York, McLaughlin Bros. (c. 1870). $12.50

10pp. text and 24pp. with illustrations printed in colors. Of different size and overlapping each other they display 13 scenes from the Blue-Beard story within a stage-like frame. In mint condition.

81. ANDERSEN (H. CHR.). Sämmtliche Märchen. Mit 125 Illustrationen von B. Pedersen. Elfte Auflage. 8vo. Original blue cloth, rebacked). Leipzig, 1870. $6.00

With 125 fine woodcut illustrations.

SHAKESPEARE, ROBINSON CRUSOE GULLIVER AND DON QUIXOTE

82. LAMB (CHARLES AND MARY). Tales from Shakespear. Designed for the Use of Young Persons. Embellished with Copper-Plates. In Two Volumes. Small 8vo. Contemporary mottled calf, red leather labels, gilt fillets on backs. (In half morocco solander slip-case). London, Thomas Hodgkins, 1807. $300.00

FIRST EDITION, first issue. With 20 full-page engravings after William Mulready.
Copies in contemporary bindings are very rare. Covers and backs of both volumes chipped, hinges broken, front cover of vol. I and back cover of vol. II loose. Otherwise fine and clean copy with good margins (pages measuring 6¾ by 4 inches). With the bookplates of Francis Wilson and his autograph signatures in upper right corner of front fly-leaves. Livington, p. 61. Ashley Library, vol. III, p. 42. Darton, Children's Books, pp. 198-99. Gumuchian, 3614.

83. THE NEW ROBINSON CRUSOE. Designed for the Amusement and Instruction of the Youth of both Sexes. Translated from the original German. Embellished with Cuts. 12mo. Original paper covered thin wooden boards, leather back (front cover defective). Hartford, John Babcock, 1800. $12.00

With 1 full-page and 11 half-page woodcuts. Spotted throughout. Except for defective binding, fair copy of a rare edition. Rosenbach lists no Robinson printed by Babcock.

84. HILDEBRANDT (C.). Robinsons Kolonie. Fortsetzung von Campe's Robinson. Ein unterhaltendes Lesebuch für Kinder. Mit dem Portrait des Herrn Rath Campe und zwey Holzschnitten von Gubitz. Small 8vo. Contemporary boards. (Back label partly missing). Leipzig, 1806. $12.00

Wilhelm Gubitz was the outstanding wood-engraver of the early nineteenth century in Germany and comparable only to Bewick. One woodcut reproduced in Rümann, Kinderbücher (plate 69).

85. ROBINSON DES ENFANTS, ou Aventures les plus curieuses de Robinson Crusoé, racontées par un père as ses enfants. Small 8vo. Original pictorial boards. Paris (c. 1850). $4.50

*With 12 attractive hand-colored engravings by Pauquet.

86. WYSS (J. R.). Der Schweizerische Robinson, oder der schiffbrüchige Schweizer-Prediger und seine Familie. Ein lehrreiches Buch für Kinder und Kinder-Freunde zu Stadt und Land. Erstes Bändchen. 8vo. Contemporary half calf, gilt fillets and labels on back. Zürich, 1812. $30.00

FIRST EDITION of volume I, which contains all that was printed in the first English edition of 1814 (see Gumuchian, 4906 and 4907). Engraved frontispiece. Of the utmost rarity. The second volume was published in 1813.

87. WYSS (J. R.). Der schweizerische Robinson . . . Erstesviertes Bändchen. Mit Kupfern. 4 vols. bound in 2. 8vo. Old half cloth. Zürich, 1851 and 1826. $18.00

Third edition of vols. I and II, first edition of vols. III and IV. With 9 full-page engravings and 1 map.

88. WYSS (J. R.). Le Robinson Suisse . . . Traduction nouvelle par Pierre Blanchard. 2 vols. 8vo. Original dark violet boards with gilt ornaments on covers and back. Paris (c. 1845). $8.50

With 8 fine full-page engravings and 1 map. Corners of one volume slightly rubbed, otherwise in fine condition.

89. VERNET (G. C.). Le Robinson Hollandais, ou Journal d'un marin naufragé. 8vo. Original printed boards, uncut. Amsterdam (1826). $6.50

With engraved pictorial title and 3 full-page engravings.

90. FAUCON (EMMA). Le Robinson Américain. Small 8vo. Original pictorial polychrome boards. Paris (c. 1850). $9.00

With 12 fine full-page lithographs by Levilly. In mint condition.

91. LEIDENFROST (CHARLOTTE). Emma der weibliche Robinson . . . Mit 4 illuminierten Kupfertafeln. Small 8vo. Pictorial boards (somewhat worn). Weimar, 1836. $6.50

*The 4 hand-colored lithographs (not engravings, as the title states) are a little clumsy but amusing and of a certain charm.

92. SWIFT (J.). Voyages de Gulliver dans les contrées lointaines. . . . Illustrée de 20 grands dessins par Bouchot. 8vo. Pictorial polychrome cloth. Paris (1843). $10.00

With 20 fine full-page woodcut illustrations.

93. (CERVANTES, MICHEL DE). The Life and Exploits of Don Quixote, de la Mancha. With the humorous Conceits of his facetious Squire, Sancho Panca. Abridged. 12mo. Original red half calf, gilt back. London, J. Harris, (Successor to E. Newbery), 1806. $15.00

With 8 full-page engravings. One of the earliest adaptions for children of this novel of world-fame that since has become a classic of the nursery. Welsh quotes a Newbery edition of c. 1798 from the publisher's list. The earliest American edition listed by Rosenbach is one of 1823. Gumuchian, 1527.

94. CERVANTES (MICHAEL). Leben und Thaten des edlen und tapfern Ritters Don Quixote von la Mancha. Zur Unterhaltung und Belustigung der Jugend neu bearbeitet von Luise Hölder. 8vo. Contemporary boards, red label. Ulm, (c. 1825). $12.00

One of the earliest adaptions for children in German. With 6 fine full-page engravings by Joh. Voltz. One plate reproduced in Rümann, Kinderbücher (plate 73).

THE MORAL TALE

95. (DAY, THOMAS). The History of Sandford and Merton. A Work Intended for the Use of Children . . . 3 vols. Small 8vo. Three-quarter calf, gilt back. London, J. Stockdale, 1784-89. $42.00

Second edition of vol. I and first edition of vols. II and III. With three engraved frontispieces, all printed here for the first time since the first edition of the first volume was published without frontispiece. Darton, Children's Books, pp. 146-48. James, Children's Books of Yesterday, p. 26 (with reproduction of title and frontispiece of vol. III).

96. SALZMANN (C. G.). Moralisches Elementarbuch, nebst einer Anleitung zum nüzlichen Gebrauch desselben. Erster Theil. Neue verbesserte Auflage. 8vo. Contemporary half calf, gilt back, blue and red label. Leipzig, 1785. $18.00

FIRST EDITION with the 68 engravings of Chodowiecki, 50 of which were copied by Blake and others for the English edition of 1791 (see No. 99 of this catalogue). With frontispiece by Rosmaesler. Some pages repaired with loss of a few words. Plate 47 is missing. Excellent proofs of the engravings. Rümann, Kinderbücher, 294.

97. A PRETTY NEW YEAR'S GIFT; or, Entertaining Histories, for the Amusement and Instruction of Young Ladies and Gentlemen, in Winter Evenings. By Solomon Sobersides . . . The First Worcester Edition. 16mo. Original blue paper boards with woodcuts on both covers. Worcester, Isaiah Thomas, 1786. $58.00

One of the earliest examples of an American publisher's ORIGINAL PRINTED BINDING. The four woodcuts, two on each cover, show different animals. With numerous woodcuts. Small piece of lower right margin of title-page torn off, not affecting the text; otherwise in excellent condition. Rosenbach, 111.

[SEE ILLUSTRATION ON PLATE VIII]

98. THE PICTURE EXHIBITION; containing the Original Drawings of eighteen disciples. To which are added Moral and Historical Explanations. Published under the Inspection of Mr. Peter Paul Rubens, Professor of Polite Arts. 16mo. Only small fragments of the original Dutch silver wrappers are preserved. Worcester, Isaiah Thomas, 1788. $38.00

No. 73

FIRST WORCESTER EDITION. With many woodcuts. The 8 pp. of advertisements at the end are present. Halsey, Forgotten Books of the American Nursery, pp. 106 and 109. Rosenbach, 134.

99. SALZMANN (C. G.). Elements of Morality, for the Use of Children; with an introductory address to parents. Translated from the German. Illustrated with fifty copper plates. In three volumes. Small 8vo. Full calf, gilt. London, J. Johnson, 1791. $38.00

FIRST EDITION. With a preface by Mary Wollstonecraft, who also translated this work from the German. With frontispiece and 50 full-page plates engraved after Chodowiecki's illustrations of the German edition (see No. 96 of this catalogue). Keynes attributes 16 plates to Blake. Gumuchian, 5092. Darton, Children's Books, 186-87.

[SEE ILLUSTRATION ON PLATE VII]

100. THE LOOKING-GLASS FOR THE MIND; or, Intellectual Mirror; being an elegant collection of the most delightful little stories and interesting tales, chiefly translated from that much admired work (by Berquin) L'Ami des Enfants. With 74 cuts, designed and engraved on wood by I. Bewick. 8vo. Contemporary calf (weak in hinges). London, E. Newbery, 1796. $15.00

The delightful woodcuts of this juvenile classic rank high among Bewick's engraved work. Reprinted in 1885 by Ch. Welsh after the 1792 edition. Gumuchian, 580.

[SEE ILLUSTRATION ON PAGE 27]

PLATE IX

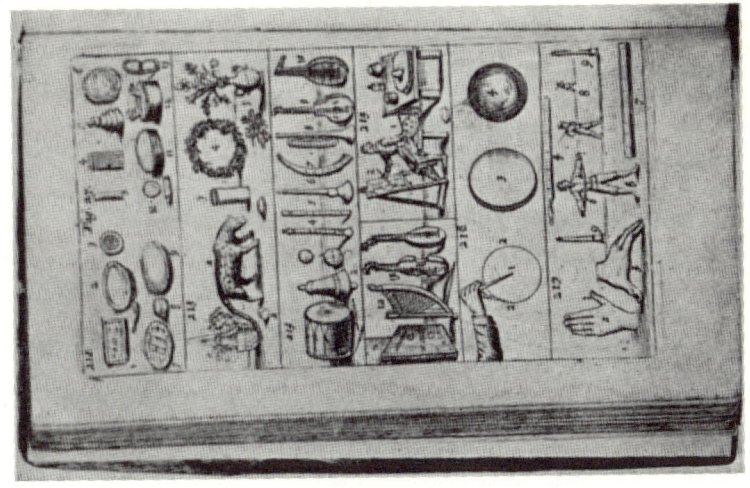

No. 31. La Porte des Langues. 1686

No. 196. Der belehrende Bergmann. 1830

PLATE X

No. 129. Hoffmann. The English Struwwelpeter. 1848

101. THE PRIZE FOR YOUTHFUL OBEDIENCE. Small 8vo. Old marbled boards, back reinforced. London, Darton and Harvey, 1800. $10.00

With 15 delightful engravings. Title-page reproduced in Tuer, Forgotten Children's Books, p. 51. First part only. The first American ediiton of the second part was published in 1803 (see **No. 104 of this catalogue**).

102. GLATZ (JAKOB). Moralische Gemälde für die gebildete Jugend. Erstes-Zweites Heft. 2 vols. 4to. Original wrappers, backstrips missing. Leipzig, 1801-03. $15.00

With the engraved portraits of Ch. G. Salzmann, author of "Elements of Morality" (see No. 99 of this catalogue), and J. Chr. Fr. Guts-Muths, author of "Gymnastics for Youth" (see No. 149 of this catalogue). In addition the work is adorned with 6 excellently engraved plates.

103. BERQUIN (ARNAUD). Oeuvres complètes. . . . 10 vols. 8vo. Contemporary half calf, gilt backs. Paris, 1802. $18.00

FIRST COLLECTED EDITION, which contains all of Berquin's writings for children, including his famous "Ami des enfants" and his translation of "Sandford and Merton." With engraved frontispiece, 189 engravings on 63 plates, 4 full-page woodcuts, and many woodcut vignettes.

104. THE PRIZE FOR YOUTHFUL OBEDIENCE. Part II. Small 8vo. Original marbled boards, label on upper cover. Philadelphia, Jacob Johnson, 1803. $10.00

With 16 woodcuts by A. Anderson. For the English edition of the first part, see No. 101 of this catalogue. Rosenbach, 289.

105. THE HOLIDAY SPY; being the Observations of Little Tommy Thoughtful, on the different Tempers, Genius and Manners, of the young Masters and Misses. . . . 16mo. Wrappers of flowered Dutch paper. London, J. Harris, 1804. $8.50

With 9 woodcuts.

[SEE ILLUSTRATION ON PAGE 1]

106. THE PICTURE ROOM; containing the Original Drawings of Eighteen Little Masters and Misses. To which are added, Moral and Historical Explanations. Published under the Inspection of Master Peter Painter, Professor of Polite Arts. The Cuts by Bewick. 16mo. Original flowered Dutch paper boards. York, T. Wilson, 1804. $13.50

With numerous woodcuts. In fine condition.

107. FUNKE (C. P.). Sittenspiegel für die Jugend. Mit zwölf Vignetten auf sechs Kupfertafeln. 8vo. Contemporary blue wrappers, uncu.t Wien, 1804. $12.50

This early manual of juvenile behavior conveys its lessons by giving examples of unpleasant characters. The fine engravings show among others: The dirty boy, the arrogant boy, the lazy boy, etc.

108. WISDOM IN MINIATURE; or, The Young Gentleman and Lady's Magazine. Being a Collection of Sentences, divine and moral. Embellished with cuts. 16mo. Original wrappers. Philadelphia, John Adams, 1805. $13.50

With frontispiece pasted down to cover and 13 woodcuts of half-page size.—Rosenbach 312.

109. LITTLE STORIES FOR LITTLE FOLKS. . . . Adorned with cuts. 16mo. Sewn. Newburyport, W. and J. Gilman, 1810 $12.00

With 10 fine woodcuts. Motto on title: "Every little Morale Tale, Shall o'er the Infant mind prevail."

[SEE ILLUSTRATION ON PAGE 33]

110. THE NEW INSTRUCTIVE HISTORY OF MISS PATTY PROUD; or, The Downfall of Vanity, with the Reward of Good-nature. 16mo. Original wrappers. New Haven, Sidney's Press, 1812. $7.50

With 10 woodcuts. The frontispiece displays Miss Proud "Showing her fine Clothes to her Play-Fellows." A device underneath reads:

> The nymph who walks the public streets,
> And sets her cap at all she meets,
> May catch the fool who turns to stare,
> But men of sense avoid the snare.

111. VILLAGE ANNALS, containing Austerus and Humanus. A sympathetic tale. Embellished with fine engravings. 12mo. Original blue wrappers. Philadelphia, Johnson and Warner, 1814. $5.50

With 7 full-page woodcuts. Rosenbach, 514.

112. MANNIGFALTIGES BILDER-UND LESE-BUCH zum Nutzen und Vergnügen für die Jugend. Small 8vo. Contemporary marbled boards. Frankfurt am Main (c. 1815). $6.50

*With 20 hand-colored engravings on 10 plates showing scenes of domestic and rural life.

113. GROOTVADER ST. JULIEN, onder zijne Kleinkinderen en hunne Speelmakkers, naar het Fransch. Met Platen. 12mo. Original printed boards. Amsterdam (c. 1815). $8.50

*Charming Dutch story-book with 8 fine hand-colored plates, including engraved title.

114. BLANCHARD (PIERRE). Les jeunes enfants. Contes. Small 8vo. Contemporary half calf, gilt fillets and red label on back. Paris (c. 1820). $6.50

Blanchard was a very prolific writer for children and his own publisher. Adorned with 6 fine full-page engravings.

115. GESPREKKEN tusschen Moeder Braafhart en hare Kinderen. Een nuttig en aangenaam Leesboekje voor de Jeugd, door eene Kindervriendin. Met Platen. Tweede Druk. 12mo. Original printed grey boards. Amsterdam, 1824. $8.50

*With 3 hand-colored engravings of an unusually fine quality. Small piece of backstrip missing, otherwise in fine condition.

116. ZAKBOEKJEN; of Letter-en Prent-Geschenk voor de Nederlandsche Jeugd. . . . Met Platen. Twede verbeterde Druk. 12mo. Original boards. Amsterdam (c. 1824). $12.50

*With 12 fine hand-colored full-page engravings depicting scenes of child life. Inserted a certificate of good behavior and industry for a little boy to whom the book was awarded.

117 VERHALEN EN LEERIJKE VOORBEELDEN VOOR DE JEUGD; benevens eenige Bijzonderheden wegens de groote en kleine Visscherijen. Met zes gekleurde Plaatjes. Small 8vo. Original yellow wrappers. Leyden, 1824. $8.50

*With fine hand-colored engravings on 6 plates, four of which illustrate Dutch fishery and whaling.

118. AKEN (F. VAN). Leerijke en aangename Gesprekken en Verhalen voor de Jeugd. Met Platen. 12mo. Original printed boards. Amsterdam (c. 1825). $10.00

*With 12 hand-colored plates illustrating the moral tales of this little Dutch story-book. One engraving shows children with their parents enjoying the spectacle of an eruption of Vesuvius by night.

119. VERTELLINGEN EN OEFENINGEN, voor Nederlandsche Kinderen. Met zes gekleurde Plaatjes. Derde Druk. Original yellow printed wrappers. Leyden, 1827. $15.00

*With engraved pictorial title-page and 5 delightful full-page engravings, both elaborately colored by hand. In mint condition, uncut and unopened.

[SEE ILLUSTRATION ON PLATE XIV]

120. LEERSAME VERTELLINGEN en deugdlievende Voorbeelden voor Kinderen; benevens eenige Merkwaardigheden uit het Rijk der Dieren. Met zes gekleurde Plaatjes. Vijfde Druk. Small 8vo. Original printed yellow wrappers. Leyden, 1827. $8.50

*With 12 hand-colored engravings, two of which show the interior of a Dutch house. The book has the autograph signature of the publisher, P. H. Trapp. In mint condition.

121. ERNSTIGE EN LUIMIGE VERHALEN in Tafereelen voor het opkomende Geslacht door C.M.D.E. Small 8vo. Original printed boards. Amsterdam, 1828. $6.50

*With hand-colored engraving on title and 2 hand-colored full-page engravings of particular charm.

122. VOORSTELLEN TER KEUZE van Ambachten en Bedijven, en daartoe betrekkelijke Verhalen voor Kinderen. Met gekleurde Platen. Vijfde Druk. Small 8vo. Original printed blue boards. Amsterdam, 1831. $7.50

*Description of 14 different trades, some of which are typically Dutch, e. g.: the ship-carpenter, the basket-maker, the peat-trampler, the Jew. The latter is presented as peddler and salesman, and the author takes occasion to defend him against unjustified prejudices. With 14 fine hand-colored engravings on 4 plates.

123. (GOODRICH, S. G.). Peter Parley's Short Stories for Long Nights. With engravings. Small 8vo. Original cloth, printed label on upper cover. Boston, Allen and Ticknor, 1834. $30.00

*Fine copy of a rare Peter Parley book with 7 delightful hand-colored full-page engravings.

[See Illustration on Page XIII]

THE PICTURE STORY

124. ROSCOE (WILLIAM). The Butterfly's Ball, and the Grasshopper's Feast. Square 12mo. Original printed tan wrappers with woodcut vignettes of a butterfly and a grasshopper (in half morocco slip-case). London, J. Harris, January 1st, 1807. $450.00

*FIRST EDITION with 14 hand-colored pictures of nearly full-page size, engraved throughout and printed on one side of the leaf only. Accompanied by the ORIGINAL PEN AND BRUSH DRAWINGS BY WILLIAM MULREADY for 12 of the engravings (preserved in a cloth-covered album, obl. 4to).

Roscoe, who was an historian and scientist, wrote this little poem for his children, supposedly as a playful account of a civic entertainment which he had attended. Like two other juvenile classics, Alice in Wonderland and Slovenly Peter, it was not originally intended for publication; but it became, as Harvey Darton says, one of the landmarks in English juvenile literature. It was the first story without any moral background, written solely for amusement's sake. It became immediately a best seller and was soon followed by a score of similar publications, the best and most successful of which was "The Peacock 'at Home.' "

This is the genuine first edition and is engraved throughout. It was reprinted in the same year from type with entirely different engravings. Tuer apparently never saw this engraved edition, for he reproduces only the typeset edition in his "Forgotten Children's Books." The only description of another copy of this engraved edition which I was able to find was that in the Gumuchian catalogue. His copy has only 12 engravings. Moreover, it differs slightly from the present copy, as the title on the printed front cover reads "Specially written for the Use of his children By Mr. Roscoe" while the present copy reads "Said to be written for . . ."

I need not emphasize the charm of the twelve original drawings by Mulready who, incidentally, at that time was only 19 years of age. They are of extraordinary artistic quality and surpass still in beauty and liveliness the fine hand-colored engravings of the book. This unique item would make the heart of every collector of children's books rejoice.

Darton, Children's Books, pp. 105-06, and plate IV, James, Children's Books of Yesterday, p. 38. Gumuchian, 4976.

[See Illustration on Plate II]

125. (DORSET, CATHERINE ANN). The Peacock "At Home." A Sequel to the Butterfly's Ball, written by a Lady. And illustrated with elegant engravings. Square 12mo. Original printed blue wrappers. London, J. Harris, Successor to E. Newbery, 1807. $13.50

First edition of this famous juvenile, the first one of many of its kind to follow Roscoe's "Butterfly's Ball" and the most successful of all of them. The 6 delightful plates, after drawings of W. Mulready, belong to the earliest work of this artist. Gumuchian, 2243. Tuer, Forgotten Children's Books, 153-55. Harvey, 206.

126. THE ADVENTURE OF LITTLE DOG TRIM and his funny Companions. Small 8vo. 16 leaves printed on one side only. Original orange wrappers, hand-colored pictorial label on front cover (preserved in half morocco case). London, G. Martin (c. 1810).
$18.50

Engraved throughout with 16 charming and amusing illustrations colored by hand. Gumuchian, 3812.

No. 100

126a. (DORSET, CATHERIN A.). Think Before You Speak; or The Three Wishes. A Tale. By the Author of "The Peacock at Home". Square 12mo. Original printed wrappers (front cover loose). Philadelphia, Johnson and Warner, 1811. $8.00

*With 6 full-page engravings. Rosenbach 438.

127. THE PRETTY, PLAYFUL, TORTOISE-SHELL CAT. A new game of questions and commands. Embellished with 14 (hand-) colored engravings. 8vo. Original orange wrappers with hand-colored decorative label on upper cover. London, Marshall, printed by D. Carvallo (c. 1825). $20.00

*The verses to one of the very amusing engravings read:
    Six Barbers dressing wigs, for a dozen learned pigs.
    Five Hens going to France, to learn a fashionable dance.
    Four Hares making a mat. Three tigers catching a rat.
    Two cows, each in a hat. With a pretty, playful tortoise-shell Cat.

128. THE KIND UNCLE AND HIS DOG GANGES. Small 8vo. Original cloth wrappers. London, Harvey and Darton, 1828. $10.00

*With 13 delightful half-page woodcuts colored by hand.

128a. THE COMIC ADVENTURES OF OLD DAME TROT and her Cat: correctly printed from the Original in the Hubbardonian Library. 8vo. Original printed linen wrappers. London (c. 1830). $6.50

*With 16 hand-colored woodcuts. Printed on one page of the leaf and each leaf linen-backed.

129. HOFFMANN (HEINRICH). The English Struwwelpeter; or, Pretty Stories and Funny Pictures for Little Children. After the Sixth Edition of the Celebrated German Work of Dr. Heinrich Hoffmann. Small 4to (9¾ by 7¾ inches). Original printed light pink boards. Leipsic (sic), Friedrich Volckmar, 1848. $600.00

*FIRST EDITION IN ENGLISH. 24 leaves printed on one side only with many hand-colored woodcuts. The title as quoted above is printed only on the front cover which therefore forms an essential part of the book.
Volckmar was the Leipzig representative of the original publisher, the Literaische Anstalt in Frankfurt am Main, for whom he handled the export business. For some reason, the details of which are not known, the name of the Literarische Anstalt does not appear on the title. But Kaysers Bücherlexikon for 1847-53 lists this edition and gives the name of the original publisher in brackets.
The pictures of the fourth German edition were still printed by means of the lithographic process. Beginning with the fifth edition, the first one to contain all the stories, the plates were printed from woodblocks. Without the bibliographical confirmation of this fact in Kayser Bücherlexikon it would be difficult to decide, on account of the excellent work of the wood-engraver, whether the pictures in this copy were taken from the stone or from woodblocks.
The English Catalogue of Books 1835-63 lists: "English Struwwelpeter Stories by Heinrich Hoffmann. London, Williams and Norgate, 1848." It may rightly be assumed (as Mr. Muir does in Notes and Queries) that the English publishers acted only as agents for the German publishing house, and the edition listed by the English cataloguer is doubtless identical with the first English edition printed in Germany and thus with our copy. The broad printed border on the covers is identical with that of the first German edition of 1845 (which, incidentally, was no longer used for the German binding after the second edition). The woodcut vignette in the center of the back cover, however, is different from that of the first German edition; it shows an old couple with two children.
The present copy is in excellent, almost mint condition. Contemporary custom-stamp in the lower right corner of the front cover. Dr. Hoffmann reports in his memoirs that he advised his publishers (rather shrewdly for a physician, one would say) to bind the books in strong boards, but to make the back of the binding very thin and fragile. Thus, he argued, the children would tear up the book pretty soon and the parents would be compelled to buy another copy! On account of this the few copies of the first German edition still in existence are rebacked. The original back-strip of the present copy is intact. It has been slightly reinforced inside the cover.
Our copy follows exactly the one described in detail by Sir H. Scott in "Notes and Queries." Since his copy lacked several leaves, the present copy is THE ONLY KNOWN COMPLETE COPY OF THE FIRST ENGLISH EDITION.
James, Children's Books of Yesterday, p. 96. Bibliographical Notes and Queries, Vol. II, Nrs. 9 and 10. Bulletin of the New York Public Library, 1933, Nr. 1.

[SEE ILLUSTRATIONS ON PLATE X]

135. GUENTHER (OTTO). Jung Purzelbaum. Eine Bärengeschichte in Bildern. Mit Reimen von Karl Fröhlich. 4to. Original hand-colored pictorial boards. Frankfurt a. M. Literarische Anstalt, Rütten und Löning (c. 1855). $15.00

*Amusing story of a little bear. With 12 hand-colored woodcuts in style similar to those of Heinrich Hoffmann's Slovenly Peter and his other picture books. At the end list of children's books, including Slovenly Peter, King Nutcracker and the poor Reynhold, etc. The title-page is reproduced in Rümann, Kinderbücher (plate 117). In mint condition. Stamp on front fly-leaf.

136. HOFFMANN (HEINRICH). Im Himmel und auf der Erde. Herzliches und Scherzliches aus dem Kinderland. 4to. Old boards, cloth back. Frankfurt a. M. (1857). $20.00

*First edition. Picture-book with amusing stories, adorned with many hand-colored woodcuts, by the author of world-famous "Slovenly Peter."

130. HOFFMANN (HEINRICH). The English Struwwelpeter; or, Pretty Stories and Funny Pictures for Little Children. . . . Thirteenth edition. 4to. Original printed brownish-red boards. Leipzig, Volckmar; London, Agency of the German Literary Society (c. 1868). $18.00

*Probably the first English edition of the revised version. The Slovenly Peter picture differs still from the final version to be found in all editions printed after 1870. The woodcuts are carefully colored by hand. The cataloguer learned recently from one of the former owners of the German publishing house that this late version was drawn under the author's supervision by a member of the artist family Klimsch.

131. (HOFFMANN, HEINRICH). Pierre l'Ebouriffé. Joyeuses Histoires et Images drollatiques. . . . Traduit par Trim. 4to. Original pictorial boards. Paris (c. 1890). $6.00

*French edttion of "Struwwelpeter." With many hand-colored woodcuts.

132. DER UNZERREISSBARE STRUWWELPETER. Allerhand Struwwelpeter-Geschichten in lustigen Reimen zur Unterhaltung und Belehrung für die lieben Kinder. Achte Auflage. 4to. Original pictorial boards. Stuttgart (c. 1860). $8.50

This picture-book is not by Heinrich Hoffmann but an imitation of his famous work. Nevertheless, the hand-colored lithographs accompanying the 8 stories are amusing and impressive.

133. MUENCHENER BILDERBOGEN. Nr. 1-480. Gr. folio. 480 sheets pasted down on both sides of 240 boards. Preserved in two portfolios. München, Braun u. Schneider (1849-1868). $150.00

*FIRST EDITION of this important series that was extended to 1200 during the following thirty years. Each sheet displays a fairy tale; a comic story (forerunner of today's comic strips); illustrations of natural history and the sciences; or costumes and fashions. The latter were later collected and published with the title "Zur Geschichte der Kostüme." The woodcuts are carefully colored by hand. The best known German artists are among the illustrators, e. g.: Schwind, Pocci, Speckter, Dietz, Muttenthaler, Braun, and, last but not least, William Busch. He has contributed 33 picture-stories, among which are some of his best. Many of the stories published in this series have set a pattern for picture-books of that time and the following decades. Some have been reprinted in other countries. W. P. Hazard in Philadelphia published a picture-book, titled "The Wonderful Chicken," which contained in recuts the Nos. 1, 5, 7, and 12. See No. 137 of this catalogue. Rümann, Kinderbücher, 40.

[SEE ILLUSTRATION ON PLATE XVI]

134. PUNCH'S MERRY PRANKS. A Little Play for Little People. 4to. Original pictorial reddish-brown boards. Leipsic, (sic) Friedrich Volckmar; London, William Tegg (c. 1850). $8.50

*Amusing Punch and Judy play. The 15 hand-colored woodcut illustrations of half- and full-page size are very funny and obviously inspired by Hoffmann's Slovenly Peter. Both books were published by the same publisher.

[SEE ILLUSTRATION ON PLATE XI]

137. THE WONDERFUL CHICKEN; and other funny Stories and Pictures. From the German. 4to. Sewn. Philadelphia, W. P. Hazard, 1860. $4.50

With many hand-colored woodcuts (see No. 133 of this catalogue).

138. HOFFMANN (HEINRICH). King Nutcracker and Poor Reynold, by Heinrich Hoffmann, author of "Slovenly Peter." Translated from the German. 4to. Marbled paper boards. Philadelphia, W. P. Hazard, 1860. $28.00

*Early American edition of the picture-book that Hoffman considered his best work. The cataloguer argrees with him and regrets that it is no longer available in today's bookshops. 24 pp. with many hand-colored woodcuts.

[SEE ILLUSTRATION ON PLATE XI]

JUVENILE FICTION

139. (KILNER, MARY JANE). The Adventures of a Pincushion. Designed chiefly for the Use of Young Ladies . . . The First Worcester Edition. 12mo. Original thin wooden boards covered with flowered paper, back-strip partly missing and covers patinated. In cloth slip-case. Worcester, Isaiah Thomas, 1788. $65.00

One of the most popular stories for children of the late 18th century. First published by Newbery of London in the same year. With many delightful woodcuts.—Rosenbach 131. Halsey, Forgotten Books of the American Nursery, page 109.

140. BRÈS (J. P.). Les Aventures du jeune Pretty. Small 8vo. Original full purple calf, blind pressed ornaments and gilt fillets on both covers and back, gilt edges. Paris (c. 1835). $18.00

*With 18 delicately engraved and brilliantly colored plates (including the pictorial title-page). Particularly fine copy in an attractive binding. Gumuchian, 907.

PLATE XI

No. 134. Punch's Merry Pranks. (C. 1850)

No. 138

PLATE XII

No. 154. Hazeu. Kinderspeelen. 1827

No. 8. Voit. Schule des Vergnügens. 1803

141. RESBECQ (ADOLPHE DE). Le Portefeuille de Polichinelle. 32mo. Original pink pictorial boards embossed and gilt, in original slip-case. Paris (c. 1840). $17.50

Engraved title and 27 delightful engravings. Gumuchian, 4727.

142. HAWTHORNE (NATHANIEL). True Stories from History and Biography. 8vo. Original red cloth, gilt back (corners and bottom of back-strip slightly chipped; top of back hinge needs small repair; otherwise sound copy). In half morocco slip case. Boston, 1851. $75.00

FIRST EDITION, first issue (Cambridge: Printed by Bolles and Houghton). 4 pp. of advertisements at the end. With 4 full-page woodcut illustrations.

143. BOZÉRIAN (JULES). Noir et Blanc. Vie et aventures de Pierrot et de son ami Arlequin. 8vo. Contemporary half morocco (somewhat rubbed and stained). Paris (c. 1855). $8.50

*With 16 hand-colored full-page lithographs by Lassalle.

144. KINGSLEY (CHARLES). The Waterbabies: a Fairy Tale for a Land-Baby. With two illustrations by J. Noel Paton. Square 8vo. Original bluish-green cloth, gilt ornament on front cover (lower part of back-strip and corners slightly chipped, light stain on front cover). London and Cambridge, Macmillan and Co., 1863. $36.00

FIRST EDITION with the rare "Envoi." Fine copy of this classic juvenile. Advertisement leaf of Chapman and Hall inserted between front fly-leaves. Darton, Children's Books, pp. 259-63. James, Children's Books of Yesterday, p. 112. Gumuchian, 3520.

145. COSMAR (A.). Schicksale der Puppe Wunderhold. Mit 8 Kupfern von Luise Thalheim. Zweite Auflage. Small square 8vo. Original boards with gilt and embossed covers (binding somewhat rubbed). Berlin, 1865. $8.50

*First edition with the delightful hand-colored lithographs by Louise Thalheim.

146. CARROL (LEWIS). Alice's Adventures in Wonderland. With forty-two illustrations by John Tenniel. 8vo. Original red cloth (some minor spots and slightly dull, but still a fine copy). In half morocco slip-case. London, 1866. $190.00

Second ediiton.

147. CARROLL (LEWIS). Through the Looking-Glass, and what Alice found there. With fifty illustrations by John Tenniel. 8vo. Original red cloth, (somewhat chipped, back-strip darkened, inner hinges cracked; fair copy). In half morocco slip-case. London, 1872. $28.00

FIRST EDITION.

148. CARROLL (LEWIS). Alice's Adventures Underground. Being a Facsimile of the original Ms. Book afterwards developed into "Alice's Adventures in Wonderland." With 37 illustrations by the Author. 8vo. Original red cloth (slightly chipped and some minor spots on covers, but on the whole a good copy). In half morocco slip-case. London, 1886. $78.00

FIRST EDITION. PRESENTATION COPY. Inscribed on half-title: "Irene Barnes from the Author Mar. 22, 1887." Irene Barnes was later the famous actress Irene Vanbrugh.

[SEE ILLUSTRATION ON PAGE 38]

148a. GREENWOOD (JAMES). The Purgatory of Peter the Cruel. With 36 illustrations, drawn on wood, by Ernest Griset. 4to. Original gilt cloth. London and New York, 1868. $10.00

*The 36 wood-engravings of full- and half-page size by Griset are carefully colored by hand. Fine copy.

GAMES AND SPORTS

149. (GUTS MUTHS, J. CHR. FR.). Gymnastics for Youth; or, A Practical Guide to Health and Amusing Exercises for the Use of Schools. An Essay toward the necessary Improvement of Education, chiefly as it relates to the body. Freely translated from the German of C. G. Salzmann, Master of the Academy of Schnepfenthal and Author of Elements of Morality. Imperial 8vo. Full calf, gilt, uncut. London, J. Johnson, 1800. $25.00

This important book is considered the foundation of modern gymnastics. Its real author was Guts Muths, who was teacher of Schnepfenthal. The first German edition of 1793 bears his name on the title-page. The attractive power of Salzmann's name as the author of "Elements of Morality" apparently induced the publisher to introduce him to the English public as the author of this work. With 9 full-page plates after the German engravings by Meil, displaying different kinds of sports, including climbing, leaping, and swimming. These plates have been attributed to Blake. A large folding plate shows gymnastic apparatuses which are still in use today. Gumuchian, 5093.

150. (GUTS MUTHS, J. CHR. FR.). Gymnastics for Youth; or, A Practical Guide to Health and Amusing Exercises. . . . Imperial 8vo. Contemporary full calf, gilt fillets and red label on back. Philadelphia, William Duane, 1802. $25.00

First American edition. Reprint of the first English edition (see No. 149 of this catalogue). The plates were reingraved in America.

151. GUTSMUTHS (J. CHR. FR.). Unterhaltungen und Spiele der Familien zu Tannenberg. Ein Taschenbuch für die Jugend. Mit 19 Kupfern. Zweite, stark vermehrte Ausgabe des Spiel-Almanchs. 12mo. Contemporary boards (chipped). Frankfurt am Mayn, 1809. $8.50

With 19 delicate full-page engravings by Ramberg depicting juvenile games, two of which are somewhat similar to today's baseball.

152. NIEUWE JONGENS-SPELEN. Met twaalf Plaatjes. 12mo. Original printed pink boards. Amsterdam (c. 1825). $10.00
Dutch book of games with 12 delightful full-page engravings. Among those shown are: stilting, lanterna magica, goat-riding, archery, etc. Mint condition.

153. BRÈS (J. P.). Les Jeudis dans le Château de ma Tante. 8 vols. Small 8vo. Original pictorial boards. Paris (c. 1825). $22.50

Each volume has a delightful engraving displaying girls in attractive costumes playing different outdoor-games. The illustrations on the bindings differ entirely from each other. One shows a balloon flying over the study of an astronomer, another a group of toys under an arcade, still another Polichinelle emerging from the clouds in front of two sphinxes. Fine set in excellent condition. Gumuchian, 914.

154. HAZEU (JOH.). Kinderspelen in leerzame Gedichtjes. Met Platen. Small 8vo. Original printed bluish boards. Amsterdam, 1827. $10.00

Dutch book of juvenile indoor- and outdoor-games. The twenty plain engravings (on 6 plates) are of great charm. In mint condition.

[SEE ILLUSTRATION ON PLATE XII]

155. DIE SPIELE DER KNABEN IN ERHOLUNGSSTUNDEN. Mit 12. fein ill. Abbild. Oblong 4to. Original hand-colored pictorial wrappers. Wien (c. 1830). $12.50

*Delightful picture-book showing children at various games. One plate displays a group of boys occupied with fowling, a "game" hardly to be recommended to children of today. The lithographed hand-colored plates show a great variety of colorful juvenile costumes. One plate reproduced in Rümann, Kinderbücher (plate 327).

156. JUGENDSPIELE zur Erholung und Erheiterung. KNABEN-SPIELE. Mit zehn illuminierten Kupfern. 12mo. Original printed boards. Tilsit (c. 1845). $8.50

157. MAEDCHENSPIELE. Same place, same date. $8.50

*The 10 hand-colored full-page plates in each volume show outdoor-games of boys and girls, respectively. In nfie condition (binding of "Mädchenspiele" a little loose).

I'd rather have a little Book, Than pies or cakes of pastry cook.

A large variety of LITTLE STORY BOOKS, of different prices, for sale at W. & J. GILMAN's Book and Stationary Store, Middle-Street, NEWBURYPORT

No. 109

158. HOUX-MARC (EUGÈNE). Les Jeux de l'Enfance. Scènes et Historiettes enfantines. Small 8vo. Pictorial chromolithographic boards (a little worn). Paris (c. 1845). $10.00

*With woodcut-vignettes and 18 lovely hand-colored engravings showing boys and girls at their games. The pictures include: blowing bubbles, blind-man's buff.skipping, etc.

159. THE AMERICAN BOY'S BOOK OF SPORTS AND GAMES. A Repository of in-and-outdoor amusements. . . . 8vo. Original pictorial blue cloth. New York (1864). $8.50

First edition of this compendium of sports, reprinted several times in the seventies and eighties. With over 600 woodcuts after White, Herrick, Wie, and Harvey. Baseball is described in extenso with six illustrations.

HISTORY AND GEOGRAPHY

160. PETIT ATLAS MODERNE ou Collection de Cartes Elementaires dédie a la Jeunesse. 4to. Contemporary full calf, gilt border on covers, gilt back, red label. Paris, 1783. $12.00

*With charming engraved pictorial title by Desrais and 27 hand-colored maps of double-page size. America is represented by 4 maps.

160a. (TRIMMER, S.). A series of Prints of Roman History, designed as Ornament for those Apartments in which Children receive the first Rudiments of their Education. Square 16mo. Contemporary full calf (rubbed and chipped). London, John Marshall, (1789). $6.00

*64 full-page engravings.

161. A NEW MORAL SYSTEM OF GEOGRAPHY, containing an account of the different nations ancient and modern . . . including a description of each country . . . adorned with the dresses of each country. The third edition, much enlarged. 12mo. Contemporary full calf. London, G. Riley, 1792. $18.00

With engraved frontispiece, folding map of the world and 57 woodcuts. The text is very instructive and tells in brief everything worthwhile to know about each country, e. g.: extent, soil, produce, trade, religion, government, climate, dresses, etc. The Americas are dealt with on pages 153-200. The woodcut symbol for the New World is a little Indian boy dressed as Amor with bow and arrow.

[See Illustration on Back Cover]

161a. THE LONDON CRIES for the Amusement of all the Good Children throughout the World. Taken from the Life. Embellished with Cuts. 16mo. Contemporary wrappers of Dutch flowered paper. Glasgow, J. and M. Robertson, 1797. $12.00

This early edition contains 26 cries, each embellished with a woodcut of almost full-page size.

162. **CAMPE (J. H.).** The Discovery of America; For the Use of Children and Young Persons. Translated from the German of J. H. Campe, Author of the New Robinson Crusoe. 3 vols. Small 8vo. Contemporary marbled boards, red leather backs. London, J. Johnson, 1799-1800. $18.00

First English edition. The first volume deals with the discovery of America by Columbus. The sub-titles of the second and third volumes, read respectively: "Pizarro: or the Conquest of Peru" and "Cortes: or the Discovery of Mexico." The work is written in the form of dialogues between a father and his children. With engraved frontispiece and three hand-colored folding maps.

163. **(SEIDEL, C. A. G.).** Gallerie der Menschen nach alphabetischer Ordnung. Ein Bilderbuch für die Jugend. . . . Mit 36 illum. Kupfern. Vierte verbesserte Auflage. Small square 8vo. Boards. Leipzig, 1801. $28.00

*The 36 delightfully hand-colored engravings show 109 different people in all walks of life in their colorful and varied costumes, e. g.: a Lady, an Amazon, a man from Florida, a Quaker, an Aviator, with his balloon, a Fool, etc., etc. One page reproduced in Rümann, Kinderbücher (plate 318).

164. **LETTERS, WRITTEN FROM LONDON,** descriptive of various scenes and occurrences frequently met with in the Metropolis and its vicinity. For the amusement of Children. Illustrated by plates. Small 8vo. Original printed wrappers (slightly soiled). London, Darton and Harvey, 1807. $12.00

With 26 engravings depicting: street-scenes; different trades; an ascending balloon; a man and two children floating in the water of the Thames and sustained by "Mr. Daniel's Life Preserver"; etc.

165. **SCHILDERUNG DER VORNEHMSTEN VOLKER** aller Weltheile oder Abenderzählungen eines Vaters unter seiner Familie von den Sitten, Gebräuchen und Gewohnheiten fremder Nationen. . . . Small 8vo. Contemporary boards. Nürnberg, 1811. $6.50

*Description of foreign countries and people in form of a dialogue between a father and his children. With 12 hand-colored costume plates.

167. **NORTHERN REGIONS;** or, Uncle Richard's Relations of Captain Parry's Voyages for the Discovery of the North-West Passage, and Franklin's and Cochrane's Overland Journeys to other Parts of the World. Small 8vo. Red leather back (gilt), original printed boards. New York, Roorbach, 1827. $12.50

With additional engraved pictorial title and 24 engravings on 12 plates. First American edition of this abridged account of the famous northern expeditions of the period. Fine copy. Another copy in medium condition is available for $6.00.

168. **PICTURE OF NEW YORK.** 16mo. Original pictorial wrappers. New York, Mahlon Day (c. 1830). $12.50

Charming booklet of 16pp. with 12 woodcuts. One of them displays the publisher's bookstore. The front cover is a replica of the title which is adorned with a vignette showing a sailboat. The text begins: "New York is a large city, containing one hundred and fifty thousand inhabitants, and twenty thousand houses. It is a thriving place." Rosenbach 745.

[SEE ILLUSTRATION ON PAGE 42]

168a. SCENES IN PARIS. Small 8vo. Original printed wrappers. London, E. Wallis, (c. 1830). $4.50

*With 12 hand-colored woodcuts. Printed on one page of the leaf only.

169. WERNBERGER (HEINRICH). Rudolph's Reise durch Europa. In getreuen Schilderungen der vorzüglichsten Städte, . . . merkwürdigsten Naturansichten, Sitten u. s. w. Ein Panorama für die heranreifende Jugend. 2 vols. Oblong 8vo. Original boards, labels. Nürnberg, 1832. $25.00

*An attractive geography for children with 33 hand-colored views of the capital cities of Europe and a hand-colored map. Rare.

170. DE WERELD IN HAAR ZONDAGSPAK. Een Geschenk voor de leergrage Jeugd. Met 16 gekleurde Platen. Small 8vo. Original green pictorial wrappers. Amsterdam (c. 1835). $10.00

*Charming Dutch costume book for children, copied after a similar English book of the same period. Except for the foreword of one page the book is engraved throughout. The delightfully hand-colored engravings are accompanied by brief poems. Two pages show North- and South-American Indians with their wives and children.

171. (GOODRICH, S.). The Child's own book of American Geography. By the Author of Peter Parley's Tales. Second edition. Small square 8vo. Original pictorial boards. Boston, 1837. $3.00

With 60 woodcuts and 18 hand-colored maps. One woodcut shows the "Baltimore Railroad," a coach on rails drawn by horses.

172. ZIEHNERT (J. G.). Bildergallerie der allgemeinen Weltgeschichte in 100 Abbildungen der wichtigsten historischen Begebenheiten, mit erläuterndem Texte. Neue Ausgabe. 8vo. Original printed boards. Meissen (c. 1840). $28.00

*The 100 brilliantly hand-colored full-page lithographs illustrate outstanding events in history of mankind, e. g.: Nebukadnezar destroys Jerusalem; Achilles kills Hector; Charlemagne visits a school; Columbus discovers America; The death of James Cook; Washington and Lafayette; etc., etc.

[SEE ILLUSTRATION ON PLATE XV]

173. (BARNUM, H. L.). Enoch Crosby; or, The Spy Unmasked. A Tale of the American Revolution. Square 12mo. Original pictorial boards, blue cloth back. Cincinnati, U. P. James (c. 1840). $7.50

Adaption for children of Barnum's well known story, based without justification on Cooper's "The Spy." With many woodcuts of half-page size. Bound in at the end initial 24 pages of another juvenile, "R. Ramble. A Book of Heroes."

174. CASTILLON (A.). Scenes et Aventures Maritimes. . . . Ouvrage dédié aux jeunes gens. 8vo. Original pictorial polychrome boards. Paris (c. 1850). $7.50

*Instructive and entertaining story of an adventurous sea voyage. With 8 hand-colored full-page engravings and many woodcut illustrations.

175. FOA (EUGÈNIE). Contes Historiques. Small 8vvo. Original half calf, printed boards. Paris (c. 1850). $4.50

*With 6 fine hand-colored lithographs by Lassalle. Two of the six stories are about Grétry, the musician, and Greuze, the painter.

176. (GOODRICH, S. G.). The Wanderers by Sea and Land, with other Tales, by Peter Parley. Illustrated with engravings. 8vo. Original cloth with polychrome ornaments. New York, Appleton & Co., 1855. $7.50

The story of the trip of two Boston children to Paris and London. With 12 full-page woodcuts, one of which shows a balloon ascension with three horses as passengers. Fine copy.

NATURAL HISTORY

177. THE NATURAL HISTORY OF BIRDS; containing a Variety of Facts selected from several writers, and intended for the Amusement and Instruction of Children. In six parts (3 vols.). Plates to the Natural History of Birds, uncolored; intended to serve the purpose of a Drawing Book for Children and Young Persons. Being the fourth volume of that work. 8vo. Contemporary full calf (some covers loose, chipped). London, 1791-92. $20.00

*With 116 delightfully hand-colored plates of European and American birds. This set is particularly rare with the fourth volume which contains an uncolored set of the engravings intended to be colored by the hand of the child.

178. DREVES (FRIEDRICH, and F. G. HAYNE). Botanisches Bilderbuch für die Jugend und Freunde der Pflanzenkunde. 4 vols. and supplement bound in 2. 4to. Contemporary marbled boards. Leipzig, 1798-1805. $24.00

*With 4 engraved pictorial title-pages and 146 hand-colored flower plates (should be 147)). The work is rare with the supplement containing the plates 133-47.

179. BILDER VATERLAENDISCHER THIERE nebst ihrer kurzen Beschreibung. Zur angenehmen und nützlichen Beschäftigung kleiner Kinder. Zweite Auflage. Small 8vo. Contemporary half morocco, gilt back. Leipzig, 1808. $20.00

*Natural history with 139 hand-colored engravings on 30 plates by Capieux, depicting animals, birds, butterflies, etc. The German text is accompanied by a French translation. With the bookplate of Czar Alexander II.

180. THE YOUTH'S CABINET OF NATURE, for the Year; containing curious Particulars characteristic of each Month. Intended to direct young people . . . 12mo. Original printed boards. New York, Samuel Wood, 1814. $7.50

With 11 half-page woodcuts. In mint condition. Rosenbach 516.

180a. THE HISTORY OF THE BIRDS IN THE AIR, designed for the amusement of all good little Boys and Girls. Ornamented with Engravings. 16mo. Original pictorial wrappers. Albany, E. and E. Hosford, 1814. $6.00

*With 21 woodcuts.

181. KLEINE NATURGESCHICHTE DER VOGEL FUR KINDER. Petite Histoire naturelle des Oiseaux à l'usage de la jeunesse. 8vo. Original pink boards, gilt back. Vienna (c. 1820). $8.50

*With eight hand-colored plates depicting 48 birds.

182. REBAU (HEINRICH). Käferbüchlein oder Beschreibung der . . . in- und ausländischen Käfer . . . für Knaben. 4to. Original pictorial boards. Reutlingen (c. 1840). $9.50

*Book about beetles. With 172 hand-colored engravings on 5 plates. The very decorative border on the front cover shows boys occupied with catching beetles and butterflies and the necessary utensils.

183. DELATTRE (CH.). Album d'histoire naturelle à la portée de la jeunesse. . . . Avec plus de cinq cent sujets de jolies gravures. Oblong small 4to. Original hand-colored pictorial boards (back reinforced). Paris, 1840. $13.50

*With over 500 carefully hand-colored engravings on 32 plates depicting: animals, birds, insects, flowers, shells, minerals and precious stones, etc., etc. The well preserved binding is very attractive.

184. MULLER (ELISABETH). Le Buffon du jeune âge. Promenades au Jardin des Plantes. Nouvelle édition. 8vo. Original pictorial polychrome boards. Paris (c. 1855). $8.00

*With ten hand-colored woodcuts and numerous smaller plain woodcut illustrations.

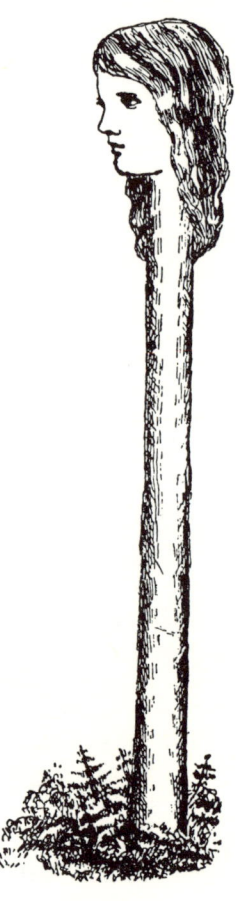

No. 148

PLATE XIII

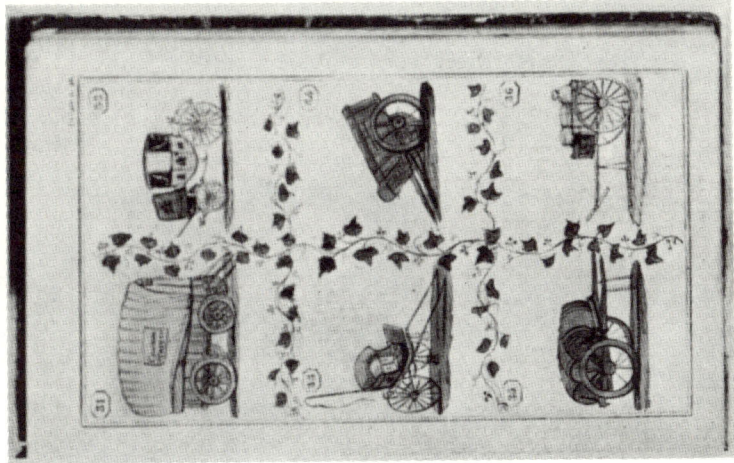

No. 40a. The Picturesque Primer. 1828

No. 123. Peter Parley's Short Stories. 1834

PLATE XIV

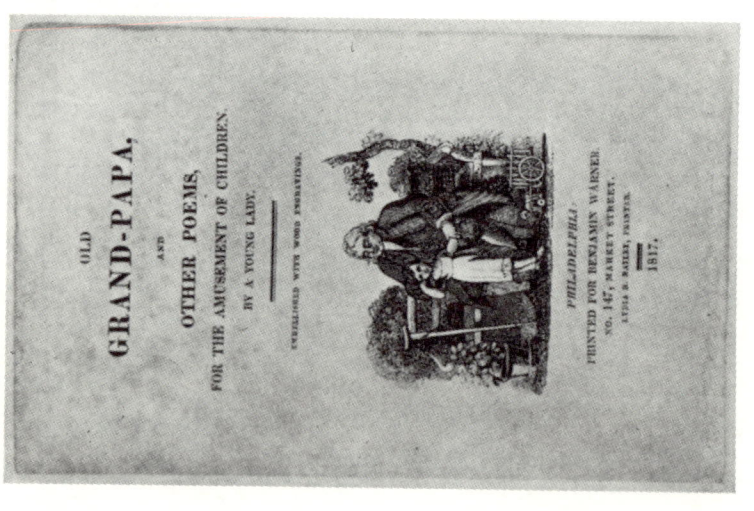

PERIODICALS AND ALMANACS

185. (WEISSE, CHR. F.). Der Kinderfreund. Ein Wochenblatt. 24 vols. bound in 8. Small 8vo. —Briefwechsel der Familie des Kinderfreundes. 12 vols. bound in 6. 8vo. Contemporary half calf, red and black leather labels, gilt backs. Leipzig, Crusius, 1777-1792. $120.00

Complete run of this famous juvenile magazine, the earliest periodical publication for children in Germany. Adorned with 36 engraved title-vignettes and 108 full-page engravings. Thes eillustrations were designed and engraved by some of the outstanding German artists of the eighteenth century as Crusius, Mechau, Schoenau, Pentzel, a. o. With numerous engraved folding music sheets.

FIRST EDITION except for vols. 1-5 of the Kinderfreund, which are present in second edition. Fine copy. Since the magazine was published over a period of 15 years complete sets in good condition and bound uniformly are difficult to find.

[SEE ILLUSTRATION ON PLATE XV]

186. STOY (JOH. SIGM.). Taschenbuch für Kinder und Kinderfreunde auf das Jahr 1781. Nürnberg, 1781. $12.00

Rare German juvenile almanac of significance because of the biographies and engraved silhouettes of 12 noted educators of the classic German period, among them: Lavater, Basedow, Campe, and Weisse who was the author of the famous children's magazine "Der Kinderfreund" (see (Nr. 185 of this catalogue). In addition there is the engraved portrait of the author and an engraving to illustrate one of the stories in the almanac. A special feature of this almanac was that the full names of the subscribing children were printed in the calendar under the date of their respective birthdays.

187. KLEINER TASCHENKALENDER AUF DAS SCHALTJAHR 1788. Mit Kupfern gezieret und mit Genehmigung der Königl. Akademie der Wissenschaften zu Berlin herausgegeben. 32mo. Contemporary blue boards. (Berlin, 1788). $8.50

The 12 delicate engravings display scenes from child life. The plate for the month of May shows two boys destroying a horn-book.

188. THE YOUTH'S MONTHLY VISITOR; or, Instructive and Entertaining Miscellany of Useful Knowledge. . . . 3 vols. 8vo. Contemporary half calf, gilt back. London, 1822-23. $18.00

*With 18 full-page engravings (10 by G. R. Cruikshank), 16 of which are colored by hand. 5 plates show reduced copies from Thornton's Temple of Flora. Many woodcuts by Bewick.

189. THE CHILDREN'S MAGAZINE. Vols. I-V. 12mo. Contemporary marbled boards, red leather backs. New York, Sunday School Union, 1829-33. $12.50

The first five volumes of an early American juvenile monthly magazine. With many woodcuts by A. Anderson a.o. The title-pages of vols. II-V are present.

190. THE JUVENILE ALMANAC; or, Series of Monthly Emblems. . . . 8vo. 26pp. Printed on one side only. Original printed pink wrapper, pictorial woodcut border on front cover. New York, Mahlon Day, 1832. $15.00

Woodcut-frontispiece by A. Anderson (signed) and 12 half-page woodcuts, apparently by the same artist, displaying the main occupations of the months of the year. Each woodcut is accompanied by a little poem, e. g., for July:

> HAY MAKING
> While the noontide sunbeams brighten,
> Maidens turn the new-mown hay;
> But, when vivid flashes frighten,
> They in terror haste away.

MISCELLANEOUS

191. HARLEQUIN SKELETON. 8vo. Old wrappers. London, R. Sayer, 1772. $18.00

Four hand-colored engravings, each with two superinposed hand-colored flaps changing the scenes. With engraved verses. Gumuchian, 2947.

192. NUMAN (H.). Tydkorting voor de jonge Jeugd, of the kinderlyk Divertissement. Bestaande in verscheide differente Figuren, in konstige Houtsnede. 8vo. Contemporary wrappers. Rotterdam (c. 1780). $12.00

Early Dutch juvenile with 29 quaint but interesting woodcuts. The first three illustrate the seasons (the spring page is missing). The next group contains pictures of domestic life. Another group of 12 woodcuts represents different types of street-musicians, peddlers, cripples, etc. The last illustration shows St. Nicholas with an umbrella on his horse. Rare.

193. HENICKE. Anweisung für deutsche Jünglinge und Mädchen in kurzer Zeit richtig zeichnen und malen zu lernen. 4to. Original pink printed covers. Leipzig, 1795. $12.50

*German drawing-book with 15 engraved plates, 9 of which are colored by hand. The last 8 plates show flowers and bouquets.

195. ZIEHNERT (J. G.). Gemälde aus dem weiblichen Geschäftskreise. Eine Bilderschule oder ein Lehrbuch über die ersten nöthigen Kenntnisse in der häuslichen Wirtschaft für junge Mädchen von 8-15 Jahren. Small square 8vo. Original cloth. Pirna (c. 1820). $8.50

*Manual of domestic knowledge for girls. With many engravings on 16 plates displaying vegetables, poultry, cattle, fish, kitchen-utensils. 5 plates are colored by hand.

196. DER BELEHRENDE BERGMANN. Ein fassliches Lese-und Bildungsbuch . . . Mit 9 schwarzen und colorirten, von C. Beichling gestochenen Kupfern. Square 12mo. Original pictorial boards. Pirna, 1830. $30.00

*Rare instructive juvenile, describing the technique of MINING and the work and life of the miner in Germany. The elaborately hand-colored engravings show the tools and machines of the miners, the scheme of a mine, and the miners in their working clothes and colorful holiday costumes.

[SEE ILLUSTRATION ON PLATE IX]

197. DIE CARNEVALS-FREUDEN oder Kleines Ideenmagazin zu geistreichen und leicht ausführbaren Masken. Mit 24 fein colorierten Kupfertafeln. Oblong 12mo. Original printed green boards with woodcut vignettes. Nürnberg, 1839. $25.00

The 24 hand-colored plates represent suggestions for amusing and phantastic fancy dresses, e. g.: magician, adults as children, rooster in boots, etc.

198. ADAM (VICTOR). Galerie pittoresque de la jeunesse. Texte de Mme. A. de Savignac et Mr. de Saintes. Oblong small 4to. Original hand-colored pictorial boards (rebacked). Paris (c. 1840). $18.00

*With 86 fine hand-colored lithographs by Adam, some of which represent: saltimbanco as dentist, a puppet-show, hunting of horses in Central America. The well preserved binding is very attractive. Gumuchian, 234.

199. BIMBACH (JULIE). Kochbüchlein für die Puppenküche oder erste Anweisung zum Kochen für Mädchen von 8-14 Jahren. Vierte unveränderte Auflage. 12mo. Original pink boards, on upper cover lithographed picture of two girls playing with a doll's kitchen. Nürnberg, 1855. $8.50

Rare COOKERY-BOOK for the doll's kitchen with about 100 miniature recipes.

200. STRAESSLE (FRANZ). Die Monate des Jahres in Bildern und Erzählungen für die liebe Jugend. Oblong 4to. Pictorial hand-colored boards. Schwäbisch-Hall (c. 1860). $8.50

*With 12 brilliantly hand-colored full-page lithographs displaying rural occupations for every month of the year. The colorful costumes are of particular charm.

THE AMERICAN WOODCUT

See items No. 11 - 12 - 13 - 19 - 24 - 27a - 28 - 52 - 53 - 57 60 - 70 - 74 - 79 - 80 - 83 - 97 - 98 - 104 - 108 - 109 - 110 - 111 137 - 138 - 139 - 142 - 159 - 168 - 171 - 173 - 176 - 180 - 180a 189 - 190.

FASHIONS AND COSTUMES

See items No. 8 - 14 - 21 - 23 - 25 - 26 - 27 - 29 - 30 - 33 - 34 35 - 40 - 42 - 51 - 80 - 96 - 99 - 107 - 112 - 115 - 116 - 122 - 133 140 - 145 - 153 - 155 - 156 - 157 - 158 - 161 - 163 - 164 - 168a 170 - 172 - 185 - 191 - 192 - 196 - 197 - 198 - 200.

BOOKS ABOUT CHILDREN'S BOOKS

201. JOHNSON (CLIFTON). Old-Time Schools and School-Books. With many illustrations collected by the Author. 8vo. Original cloth. New York, 1904. $6.00

Original edition. A reprint was made in 1935.

202. DARTON (F. J. HARVEY). Children's Books in England. Five Centuries of Social Life. Royal 8ov. Original cloth. Cambridge, 1932. $4.00

An excellent scholarly study and the best book on the subject, indispensable to the collector of English and American children's books. With 8 plates.

203. HALSEY (ROSALIE V.). Forgotten Books of the American Nursery. A History of the Development of the American Story-Book. Royal 8vo. Original boards, cloth back. Boston, 1911. $6.00

This book should be on the shelf of every collector of early American children's books. With 25 plates.

204. JAMES (PHILIP). Children's Books of Yesterday. 4to. Original cloth. London and New York, 1933. $2.00

With numerous illustrations on 112 pages.

205. ROSENBACH (A. S. W.). Early American Children's Books. With Bibliographical Descriptions of the Books in his Private Collection. Foreword by A. E. Newton. 4to. Original half morocco, pictorial boards. Portland, 1933. $25.00

Limited edition. With 104 plates, partly colored by hand.

206. RUMANN (ARTHUR). Alte Deutsche Kinderbücher. Royal 8vo. Original cloth. Vienna, 1937. $8.00

With 150 plates, 8 of which are in colors.

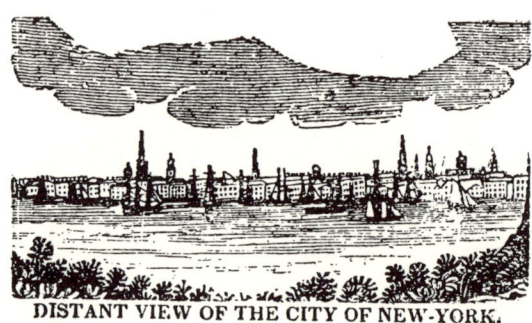

No. 168

The books offered in this catalogue are only a selection from my stock of early children's books. I would be glad to answer any inquiry regarding your special interests.

PLATE XV

No. 172. Ziehnert. Bildergallerie. (C. 1840)

No. 185

PLATE XVI

133. Münchener Bilderbogen. 1849-68
(Considerably reduced)

INDEX

ABC	2, 3, 16
Abécédaire	17
Adam (V.). Galerie pittoresque	198
Adventure of little dog Trim (The)	126
Aesop. Fables	61, 70, 77a
Aken (F. v.). Leerijke enangename Gesprekken	118
Alphabet caricature	25
Alphabet récréatif	10
Alphen (H. v.). Kleine Gedichten	54
American Boy's Book of Sports and Games (The)	159
Andersen (H. Chr.). Sämtliche Märchen	81
Andersen (H. Chr.). Story Book	74
Andersen (H. Chr.). Wonderful Tales	79
A was an Apple	19
Barnum (H. L.). Enoch Crosby	173
Belehrende Bergmann (Der)	196
Bertin (T. P.). Le Passe Temps de l'Enfance	35
Berquin (A.). The Looking-Glass for the Mind	100
Berquin (A.). Oeuvres complètes	103
Bijbelsch Prentgeschenk voor Kinderen	48
Bilder—ABC	4
Bilder Vaterländischer Tiere	179
Bimbach (J.). Kochbüchlein für die Puppenküche	199
Blanchard (P.). Les jeunes enfants	114
Bloemen en Bladen	26
Blue-Beard	80
Bozérian (J.). Noir et Blanc	143
Brès (J. P.). Les Aventures du jeune Pretty	140
Brès (J. P.). Les Jeudis dans le Château de ma Tante	153
Campe (J. H.). ABC instructive	7
Campe (J. H.). The Discovery of America	162
Campe (J. H.). The new Robinson	83
Campe (J. H.). Robinson des Enfants	85
Carnevals-Freuden (Die)	197
Carroll (L.). Alice's Adventures in Wonderland	146
Carroll (L.). Alice's Adventures Underground	148
Carroll (L.). Through the Looking Glass	147
Castillon (A.). Scenes et Aventures Maritimes	174
Cervantes (M.). Don Quixote	93, 94
Children's Magazine	189
Child's Illuminated Alphabet	24
Collection of Pretty Poems (A)	49
Comic Alphabet (The)	20
Cosmar (A.). Schicksale der Puppe Wunderhold	145
Court of Oberon (The)	65
Cruikshank (G.). Fairy Library	77
Curieuse Bilder-Bibel	45
Curious Hieroglyphick Bible (A)	46
Darton (F. J. H.). Children's Books in England	202

Day (Mahlon). Miscellaneous Juveniles 57
Day (Th.). The History of Sandford and Merton 95
Delattre (Ch.). Album d'histoire naturelle 183
Dreves (F.). Botanisches Bilderbuch 178
Dorset (C. A.). The Peacock "At Home" 125
Dorset (C. A.). Think before you speak 126a
Eberhard (G. A.). ABC und Lesebuch 6
Eenige Voorstellingen van Natur 38
Emy. Alphabet illustré 27
Ernstige en Luimige Verhalen 121
Faucon (E.). Le Robinson Américain 90
Festkalender 59
Fletcher (W.). The Picturesque Primer 40a
Foa (E.). Contes Historiques 175
Food for the Mind 52
Funke (C. Ph.). Familien-Bilder-Buch 37
Funke (C. Ph.). Sittenspiegel für die Jugend 107
Gailer (J. E.). Neuer Orbis Pictus 41
Gesprekken tusschen Moeder Braahart 115
Glatz (J.). Moralische Gemälde 102
Goodrich (S. G.). The Child's Book of American Geography 171
Goodrich (S. G.). Peter Parley's Short Stories 123
Goodrich (S. G.). The Wanderers by Sea and Land 176
Greenaway (K.). Alphabet 30
Greenaway (K.). An Apple Pie 29
Greenwood (J.). The Purgatory of Peter the Cruel 148a
Grimm (A. L.). Märchen-Bibliothek 64
Grimm (W. and J.). German Popular Stories 66
Grootvader St. Julien 113
Günther (O.). Jung Purzelbaum 135
Gutmann (J.). Leseconfect 23
Guts Muths (J. Ch. F.). Gymnastic for Youth 149, 150
Guts Muths (J. Ch. F.). Unterhaltungen und Spiele 151
Halsey (R.). Forgotten Books of the American Nursery 203
Harlequin Skeleton 191
Hawthorne (N.). True Stories 142
Hazeu (J.). Fabelen uit het Dierenrijk 67
Hazeu (J.). Kinderspelen 154
Henicke. Anweisung . . . richtig zeichnen zu lernen 193
Hildebrandt (C.). Robinsons Kolonie 84
History of an Apple Pie 18
History of the Birds 180a
Hoffmann (H.). The English Struwwelpeter 129, 130
Hoffmann (H.). Im Himmel und auf der Erde 136
Hoffmann (H.). King Nutcracker and Poor Reynold 138
Hoffmann (H.). Pierre l'Ebouriffé 131
Holiday Spy (The) 105
House that Jack built (The) 58
Houx-Marc (E.). Les Jeux de l'Enfance 158
Illustrated ABC (The) 27a
James (Ph.). Children's Books of Yesterday 204

Johnson (C.). Old-Time Schoolbooks ... 201
Juvenile Almanac (The) ... 190
Juvenile Numerator (The) ... 51
Kern und Auszug des Buches Jesus Sirach ... 44
Kilner (M. J.). The Adventures of a Pincushion ... 139
Kimber and Conrad's ABC Book ... 11
Kind Uncle and his dog Ganges (The) ... 128
Kingsley (Ch.). The Waterbabies ... 144
Kleine Bilder-Bibel für Kinder ... 47
Kleine Fabelwelt für kleine Leute ... 63
Kleine Naturgeschichte der Vögel für Kinder ... 181
Kleiner Taschenkalender ... 187
Knabenspiele ... 156
Lamb (Ch. and M.). Tales from Shakespeare ... 82
Lederer (J. G.). Der kleine Lateiner ... 34
Leerzam Tijdverdrijf ... 39
Leersame Vertellingen ... 120
Leidenfrost (Ch.). Emma der weibliche Robinson ... 91
Letters written from London ... 164
Little Stories for Little Folks ... 109
Livre des Enfants (Le) ... 69
London Cries (The) ... 161a
Mädchenspiele ... 157
Mannigfaltiges Bilder- und Lese-Buch ... 112
Märchen und Sagen ... 78
Martin (W.). The Parlour Book ... 43
Meynier (J. H.). Neuer Orbis Pictus ... 40
Milles et Une Nuit (Les) ... 72
Monroe's Primary Reading Charts ... 28
Mother Bunch's Fairy Tales ... 62
Mother Goose's Melodies ... 60
Müller (E.). Le Buffon du jeune âge ... 184
Münchener Bilderbogen ... 133
Musäus (J. K. A.). Volksmärchen der Deutschen ... 73
Natural History of Birds (The) ... 177
Neuer Orbis Pictus ... 82
Neue systematische Bilderschule ... 42
New England Primer (The) ... 12, 13
New instructive History of Miss Patty Proud (The) ... 110
New Moral System of Geography (A) ... 161
Nieuwe Jongens-Spelen ... 152
Northern Regions ... 167
Nouvelle Méthode d'enseigner l'ABC ... 5
Numan (H.). Tydkorting voor de jonge Jeugd ... 192
Old Dame Trot (The comic adventure of) ... 128a
Old Grand-Papa ... 53
Perrault (Ch.). Les Contes des Fées ... 75, 76
Petit Atlas moderne ... 160
Picture Exhibition (The) ... 98
Picture of New York ... 168
Picture Room (The) ... 106
Porte des Langues ... 31

Pretty New Year's Gift (A)	97
Pretty Playful Tortoise-Shell Cat (The)	127
Prize for Youthful Obedience (The)	101 104
Progress of Industry (The)	58a
Punch's merry pranks	134
Rebau (H.). Käferbüchlein	182
Reinhardt (J. G.). Nieuw en volkomen ABC	15
Resbecq (A. de). Le Portefeuille de Polichinelle	141
Roscoe (W.). The Butterfly's Ball	124
Rosenbach (A. S. W.). Early American Children's Books	205
Rümann (A.). Alte Deutsche Kinderbücher	206
Salzmann (C. G.). Elements of Morality	99
Salzmann (C. G.). Moralisches Elementarbuch	96
Sammlung von Fabeln	68
Scenes in Paris	168a
Schilderung der vornehmsten Völker	165
Schoppe (A.). Kleines Schatzkästlein	21
Seidel (C. A. G.). Gallerie der Menschen	163
Seidel (H.). Neuer Orbin Pictus in sechs Sprachen	36
Selbiger (F.). Neues ABC, Lese- und Unterhaltungsbuch	14
Sneewittchen	71
Songs for the Nursery	174
Spiele der Knaben in Erholungsstunden (Die)	155
Splittegard (C. F.). Neues Bilder ABC	9
Strässle (F.). Die Monate des Jahres	200
Stoy (J. M.). Taschenbuch für Kinder	186
Swift (J.). Voyages de Gulliver	92
Tabulae Abcdariae Puerilis	1
Trimmer (S.). A series of prints of Roman History	160a
Unzerreissbare Struwwelpeter (Der)	132
Vaterlandsch A. B. Boek	182
Verhalen en leerijke Voorbeelden voor de Jeugd	117
Vernet (G. C.). Le Robinson Hollandais	89
Vertellingen en Oefeningen	119
Village Annals	111
Vois (J. P). Schule des Vergnügens	8
Voorstellen ter Keuze	122
Watts (I.). Divine Songs	50
Weisse (Ch. F.). Der Kinderfreund	185
Wereld in haar Zondagspak	170
Wernberger (H.). Rudolphs Reise durch Europa	169
Wisdom in Miniature	108
Wonderful Chicken (The)	137
Wyss (J. R.). Le Robinson Suisse	88
Wyss (J. R.). Der Schweizerische Robinson	196, 197
Youth's Cabinet of Nature (The)	180
Youth's Monthly Visitor (The)	188
Zakboekjen	116
Ziehnert (J. G.). Bildergallerie der allgemeinen Weltgeschichte	172
Ziehnert (J. G.). Gemälde aus dem weiblichen Geschäftskreise	195

COUNTRIES OF ORIGIN

AMERICAN

11	28	60	83	110	138	168	180
12	52	66	97	111	139	171	180a
13	53	70	98	113	142	173	189
19	55	74	104	123	150	176	190
24	57	79	108	126a	159		
27a	58	80	109	137	167		

DUTCH

7	26	39	67	116	119	122	170
15	31	48	89	117	120	152	192
22	38	54	115	118	121	154	

ENGLISH

18	46	65	99	124	129	148	164
20	49	77	100	125	130	148a	168a
29	50	77a	101	126	134	149	177
30	51	82	103	127	144	160a	188
40a	58a	93	105	128	146	161	161a
43	62	95	106	128a	147	162	191

FRENCH

5	25	61	76	90	140	158	183
7	27	69	85	92	141	160	184
10	31	72	88	114	143	174	198
17	35	75	89	131	153	175	

GERMAN

2	21	41	68	87	133	163	185
3	23	42	69	91	135	165	186
4	32	44	71	94	136	169	193
6	33	45	73	96	145	172	195
8	34	47	78	102	151	178	196
9	36	59	81	107	155	179	197
14	37	63	84	112	156	181	199
16	40	64	86	132	157	182	200

No. 161